I0797790

Advance Praise for *Big Talk*

"In a world where so many of us are struggling to find the right words, *Big Talk* is the answer. It shows us how to move past the awkward, break through the noise, and discover the joy of genuine human connection. A powerful reminder that conversations can change our lives."

—Jay Shetty, #1 *New York Times* bestselling author and host of the *On Purpose* podcast

"In the midst of a loneliness epidemic, *Big Talk* feels like a cure—a simple, human reminder that connection can start with a single honest question. Kalina does an amazing job at showing how to replace empty exchanges with conversations that matter—ones that build trust, understanding, and belonging. This isn't just a book about conversation; it's a guide to feeling human again."

—Hunter Prosper, *New York Times* bestselling author of *Stories from a Stranger*

"Finding real connection with others doesn't have to be complicated. Everyday interactions, along with genuine curiosity and an open mind, are often all it takes to foster trust. This book shows us how."

—Nedra Glover Tawwab, *New York Times* bestselling author of *Set Boundaries, Find Peace*

"*Big Talk* is a breath of fresh air. Reading this book feels like sitting down with a good friend. Kalina writes with so much warmth and honesty, you can't help but be inspired and learn how to move past the surface and connect in a real way. *Big Talk* is the reminder we all need that we're meant for deeper conversations."

—Julie McFadden (Hospice Nurse Julie), *New York Times* bestselling author of *Nothing to Fear*

"In a clickbait, small-talk world, *Big Talk* dares us to go deeper and connect authentically. Kalina Silverman shares powerful stories and a clear framework to transform everyday moments into real connections—around the water cooler, at the dinner table, at a neighborhood park—anywhere life happens. This book is your invitation to speak with strangers, listen with your soul, and create conversations that last a lifetime!"

—Shaka Senghor, *New York Times* bestselling author of *Writing My Wrongs* and *How to Be Free*

"True connection is what we want most—and yet, in today's world, it can be incredibly challenging to find and cultivate. In this powerful and practical guide, Kalina Silverman helps lead us back to one another and, in the process, to better lives and a better world. Packed with inspiring stories and actionable strategies, *Big Talk* is a book we can all put to good use."

—Stephanie Harrison, international bestselling author of *New Happy*

"Kalina Silverman's *Big Talk* revives the lost art of conversation and curiosity—not just asking what someone does but how they feel about what they do, revealing who they really are. This book is the tool kit we need to unlock all the beauty hiding in plain sight."

—Steve Goldbloom, creator of the Emmy-nominated series "Brief But Spectacular," airing on *PBS NewsHour*

"Kalina Silverman's positivity is infectious! I've been so impressed and inspired by her uniquely hopeful perspective on our shared humanity. This uplifting book will give you the jolt of optimism you've been craving as it lays out her highly relatable methods for creating deeper and more meaningful experiences in life and relationships. This is the book the world desperately needs right now."

—Ryan Dusick, founding drummer of Maroon 5, licensed therapist, and author of *Harder to Breathe*

"Studies show us that deep connection is the salve for loneliness and that one in four Americans say they don't have someone to confide in. This makes *Big Talk* a much-needed, nonnegotiable skill for solving the loneliness epidemic. It's deep conversation that makes us feel more connected. This incredible book gives you practical strategies for getting to deeper conversation more quickly."

—Simone Heng, award-winning author of *Let's Talk About Loneliness*

"Kalina Silverman blends authentic storytelling with social impact, helping us see ourselves—and one another—through a more honest and compassionate lens. *Big Talk* is a refreshing antidote to small talk, sparking the kinds of conversations that heal, inspire, and create real change. Having seen the ripple effect of Kalina's work firsthand, I know her message has the power to transform not just how we communicate, but how we connect as humans."

—Erin Raftery Ryan, CEO, NAMI (National Alliance on Mental Illness) of Westside Los Angeles

Big Talk

How to Skip Small Talk, Make Meaningful Connections, and Enrich Your Life

Kalina Silverman

TARCHER
an imprint of Penguin Random House
New York

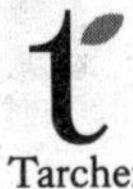

an imprint of Penguin Random House LLC
1745 Broadway, New York, NY 10019
penguinrandomhouse.com

Book design by Daniel Brount

ISBN 9780593855317
Ebook ISBN 9780593855331

Printed in the United States of America
1st Printing

The authorized representative in the EU for product safety and compliance is Penguin Random House Ireland, Morrison Chambers, 32 Nassau Street, Dublin D02 YH68, Ireland, https://eu-contact.penguin.ie.

To my grandfather, who treated everyone in the world like a friend and neighbor

CONTENTS

PREFACE

The Big Talk Story

The world is full of lonely people afraid to make the first move.

—TONY LIP, *GREEN BOOK*

When I started broadcast journalism school in 2012, I dreamed of becoming an international TV newscaster, reporting breaking stories and connecting the world. But I quickly realized that traditional news prioritized deadlines and headlines over real human connection. To me, the true heart of a story wasn't just in the facts—it was in people's emotions and the depth of their experiences.

My appetite for adventure then turned to war reporting. I aspired to be like Lynsey Addario, going undercover to report on the Taliban,[1] and Dan Eldon, driving across Africa, documenting hard-hitting realities on the ground, and embracing safari as a way of life.[2] I was drawn to stories that revealed emotional extremes—courage, hope, and camaraderie amid devastation. I wanted to follow in their footsteps to the front lines of major global events, in search of deep truths about humanity.

Then, in 2014, my perspective changed. James Foley, an alumnus of my school, was abducted and killed while reporting in Syria. His loss was a sobering and heartbreaking reminder of the real risks war correspondents face.

That tragedy forced me to rethink my path. Did I need to document the devastation of war to explore the depths of human experience? Or was there another way?

So I asked: *What if I could help foster empathy and connection before conflicts arise? What if I could share stories that celebrate our shared humanity to build bridges of understanding?*

These questions laid the foundation for Big Talk.

Big Talk's Early Days

I come from three generations of doctors, starting with my Hawaiian-born great-grandmother, whose father was an ambassador to the last king of Hawaii. My mixed-race family eventually landed in Southern California for my parents' medical residencies.

Growing up in Santa Monica with doctors for parents and diplomats and educators for ancestors, I developed a love for helping others, a curiosity about humanity, and a spiritual appreciation for the mountains and sea. But while my family often discussed medical maladies over the dinner table, I knew early on that my path lay elsewhere.

When I joined my family on a medical volunteer trip to Cambodia, I was more interested in interviewing doctors and local patients than in witnessing hospital procedures. I craved more opportunities to meet new people and explore faraway worlds. That experience led me to Northwestern University to pursue a degree in broadcast journalism.

When I left sunny Southern California at age eighteen to move across the country to Illinois, my world clouded—literally and figuratively. Despite meeting many new people, I felt surprisingly lonely and disconnected from my surroundings. Back home, my childhood friends came from broad cultural backgrounds and interests. But in college, I noticed people seeking comfort in sameness. I couldn't understand this difference. I longed for the easygoing, diverse connections I had grown up with.

I felt detached from my new world. Despite being surrounded by people every day, I came home in the evenings with a confusing sense of emptiness. I was ashamed of my feelings and didn't tell a soul, fearing I would seem weak and strange.

I took up swimming. Where no one could see me, I felt the freedom to let my tears flow underwater.

My friends back home thought I was having the time of my life. They saw photos on social media of me and my new friends with our arms happily thrown around each other. But that's not how I felt.

In my journal, I wrote:

> I wish I could start my first entry with an ecstatic story about how my new life is going, but since this is a personal journal, I can be honest and say I've never remembered feeling more lost in my entire life, and only three-quarters know that everything will work out and I'll be OK. I miss home and being surrounded by people who know me well and love me for all I am.

Throughout my first year of university, the question plagued me: "*Who am I?*" I thought I had lost my identity.

Thankfully, the sun came out again. At the end of the year, I opened up to those around me about what I'd been through and asked my friends to share their stories of struggle for a journalism piece I was writing. I was shocked by how many people wrote back! So many had gone through the same thing I had, but we just didn't discuss it.

That's when I realized that believing I was alone in feeling lonely was actually what had been keeping me from feeling happy and connected.

One evening, I came home late from a party and hopped on a video chat with a faraway friend. We had a thoughtful and heartfelt conversation. I exclaimed, "Wow, I wish more conversations were like this!" He said, "Yeah, screw small talk."

His statement was a revelation. I wondered: *What if we could skip small talk when talking to our friends, classmates, coworkers, or even strangers and instead discuss the things that really matter in life—the things that we genuinely care about and want to discuss?*

So, I considered: *How about we find ways to skip the small talk and instead "make big talk"?*

I didn't immediately know what to do with the phrase "Big Talk" that had come to my mind, so I tucked it away.

I started to venture outside of my comfort zone. On one occasion, I took the train to the South Side of Chicago when it was 16 degrees outside. I stood outside in the cold to talk to people about income disparities and their struggles. Despite my toes nearly freezing from frostbite, I was thrilled and motivated by the conversations I had. I was inspired to continue stepping outside my usual world, going to places where impactful stories unfold, and listening with empathy.

The following summer, through my journalism program, I had the opportunity to work on an international documentary project. I spent three magical weeks in Ecuador working with a team of bright young women on a documentary about education reform. Whether gliding down the Amazon River, climbing the Andes Mountains, or salsa dancing through the streets of Cuenca, we often stopped to meet and interview new people. Every day was a serendipitous adventure!

I pondered: *Why do we experience life more vividly when traveling than when living at home? Is it because we are too preoccupied with ourselves in everyday life and unable to look outward?*

While away from home, I knew that my mentality and approach invited more magical encounters into my everyday experiences. Toward the end of my trip, I started to dread returning to reality. I wondered how I could make everyday life feel as meaningful.

During one more opportunity to go abroad that summer, I went to Germany to work on a story about the Holocaust. On one of my last days there, I came upon a question scratched onto the Berlin Wall: "*What do you want to do before you die?*" This question lit a spark in me.

I came home from Germany five weeks before starting my junior year of college with a resolve to try an experiment. I took the question from the Berlin Wall, the inspiration from traveling and talking with strangers, as well as the video chat with my friend, and set out on a personal social experiment.

I called it *Big Talk*.

For six weeks, I walked up to strangers around Los Angeles with my video camera. I skipped small talk by introducing myself and asking them two questions: "What do you want to do before you die?" and "What would you do if you knew you were going to die tomorrow?" Here are some of their answers:

- "Take a road trip to see someone and tell them I love them." —A woman toweling off after a morning dip in the sea.
- "Travel the Appalachian Trail." —A man experiencing homelessness resting by a pier with his dog. He told me he hadn't seen his two children in a long time.
- "Go to the priest and make a confession." —An Italian man painting on the bluffs en plein air. I saw him again five years later, during the global pandemic, still painting.
- "I would love to have my dog on my bed with me." —An elderly woman I met outside my late grandmother's apartment. Three years later, I ran into her again, and we talked about love and loss.
- "See my kids graduate. I spend too much time working." —A businessman late to work in Beverly Hills. He teared up as he shared that his mother had been asked the same question the night before she passed away.

By asking two questions and "making Big Talk," I learned more about the life stories of complete strangers and developed more meaningful connections with them than if I had just passed them by or made small talk.

I filmed my conversations with these once-strangers and published the video on YouTube. It went viral through coverage by global news outlets and led to a TEDx talk, "How to Skip the Small

Talk and Connect with Anyone."[3] Afterward, messages came pouring in from people worldwide who wanted to "join the Big Talk movement."

I was inspired to find ways to expand Big Talk beyond my immediate community and personal encounters, so I continued to give talks and created a "Big Talk Question Card Game" to help people make Big Talk in their own lives.

Stories began to flow in from people who Big Talk impacted:

- A woman messaged: "The Big Talk video saved my life. When asking myself, 'What do I want to do before I die?' I realized I must quit smoking before it's too late for me and my family."
- A Los Angeles Lakers G League team coach told me about using Big Talk cards on a bus ride with his team: "The questions brought us closer as teammates, and now we have guys requesting to make Big Talk on the road."
- International models from Germany and Thailand reached out: "In the modeling industry, there's a lot of shallowness. We need more depth there, so we started hosting Big Talk pizza dinners to get to know one another on a deeper level."
- Harvard Medical School used the original Big Talk video and questions for three years of orientations to inspire future doctors to lead with communication and empathy.

While Big Talk was gaining international attention, I still needed to make a living, so I took a temp job as a receptionist for three months. I used that time, sitting all day behind a desk in a dimly lit room, to apply for a research grant.

It paid off, and I was awarded a Fulbright scholarship from the U.S. Department of State and the Institute of International Education to move to Singapore for a year to study ways to establish empathy through Big Talk. There, I led workshops with Singaporeans, migrant workers, and expats and tested different questions that people could relate to across cultures. My research in Singapore led me to present Big Talk workshops to companies and schools in regions as distant as Australia and Uzbekistan.

When I came back to America, I developed a Big Talk model that has served as the basis of workshops I've conducted with groups of people ranging from elementary through college students, as well as army veterans, tech entrepreneurs, corporate professionals, psychologists, artists, government workers, and entertainers—always challenging myself and others to reflect on the question:

"How can I take what I learned today to make my life different tomorrow?"

Through Big Talk, I found my answer to how to inspire change through storytelling and connection. I've always sought stories that reveal emotional extremes—courage, hope, and resilience through adversity. But I realized I didn't need to look to distant, dangerous, or dramatic settings to find them and to advocate for peace or have a social impact.

The most transformative moments happen every day, everywhere. I could still illuminate humanity's beauty, struggles, and truths by venturing into whatever communities I found myself in, having meaningful conversations, and sharing those exchanges.

People worldwide have described how Big Talk has impacted their lives. A prisoner serving a life sentence found hope and connection through Big Talk conversations in his psychiatric ward. An army captain used Big Talk to strengthen his long-distance relationship, leading to a marriage proposal. In fact, on two occasions, people have reached out asking for a custom "Will you marry me?" Big Talk Question Card because the questions had such a profound impact on their relationships. One man wrote to say that he got to know his girlfriend (now wife) through Big Talk. He attached a photo of their baby girl and added, "Thank you for your butterfly effect."

A man with autism who encountered Big Talk learned to better express his thoughts openly to his family. A single mother made Big Talk questions a bedtime ritual with her six-year-old daughter. In early 2025, when fires devastated entire neighborhoods in Los Angeles, I met with survivors to make Big Talk and share their stories of loss and hope, helping to raise over $2 million for them.

Thank you to everyone who has shared their stories, experiences, and vulnerabilities on this journey. Some have moved me to tears, and others have reaffirmed how a simple exchange—on a walk by the sea or outside a coffee shop—can be life-changing.

This book is the culmination of those experiences, research, and insights. This book is for those who find poetry, beauty, and meaning in daily interactions. It's also a practical guide for busy people seeking tools to deepen their relationships. It blends actionable strategies for skipping small talk with reflections on how we can better understand and relate to one another.

Over the years, I've personally made Big Talk with thousands of people and led interactive Big Talk workshops for tens of thousands of others.

The Big Talk conversations and workshops are the foundation of this book. I hope it helps you move beyond small talk to find greater depth, beauty, and connection in the everyday conversations that shape our lives.

—Kalina Silverman

INTRODUCTION

Why Skip Small Talk?

I wonder how many people I've looked at all my life and never seen.

—JOHN STEINBECK, *THE WINTER OF OUR DISCONTENT*

My motto since overcoming loneliness and embracing a life of Big Talk is inspired by the film *Into the Wild*, when Christopher McCandless realizes, after living in social isolation for 114 days, "Happiness is only real when shared."[1]

Starting a genuine conversation may feel nerve-racking, but the absolute risk lies in avoiding it—missing the chance to form deeper connections and instead facing loneliness. In fact, social isolation and loneliness are critical social determinants of health, just like obesity, lack of exercise, and smoking.[2]

The former surgeon general of the United States, Dr. Vivek Murthy, said loneliness is considered as lethal as smoking fifteen cigarettes a day,[3] and a study from the National Institute on Aging found loneliness and social isolation can increase the risk of premature death by 50 percent.[4] Loneliness isn't just an American problem.

The United Kingdom introduced a new ministry position—the "Minister for Loneliness"—in 2018.[5] Similarly, Japan welcomed its first Minister of Loneliness in 2021.[6]

The rise in loneliness may be attributed to our virtual tech-driven culture, Western individualism, and the decline of tight-knit communities. Since the mid-twentieth century, more people have been living alone, making it harder to form those natural, deep connections in everyday life.[7]

Big Talk helps create those deep connections between people. When you ask profound questions and listen compassionately, you can witness someone's heart crack open. And it's in those moments when a person opens up, sharing a lost dream, a hidden fear, or a lonely struggle, that true understanding and empathy flow between you.

We often think we have to face life's anxieties alone, but it's better to go through them together. Anna Draper's words in the show *Mad Men* resonate: "The only thing keeping you from being happy is the belief that you are alone."[8] The key to true happiness and fulfillment is our connections with others. It's what ultimately matters in life. Dr. Murthy stated:

> When I think back on the patients I cared for in their dying days, the size of their bank accounts and their status in the eyes of society were never the yardsticks by which they measured a meaningful life. What they talked about were relationships. The ones that brought them great joy. The relationships they wish they'd been more present for. The ones that broke their hearts. In the final moments, when only the most meaningful strands of life remain, it's the human connections that rise to the top.[9]

I can't recall many small talk conversations. On the other hand, I can vividly recall Big Talk conversations with strangers and friends alike from years ago. Big Talk makes conversations more memorable and can even change or save lives. After I have a Big Talk conversation, I am often bursting with gratitude, genuine joy, and awe for humanity.

One of the reasons I created Big Talk was because I wanted real life to feel as vivid, emotional, and triumphant as reading a captivating book or watching a moving film. I was tired of finishing an epic story, only to experience that post-book or post-movie "hangover"—the letdown of returning to a reality that felt dull by comparison.

Big Talk became my way of bringing that sense of depth and meaning into everyday life—proving that real moments, when shared with honesty and intention, can be just as moving as fiction.

The next time you meet someone, ask them a Big Talk question. Ask about their childhood, dreams, biggest regrets, and life lessons. You might be surprised by what you learn, not just about them but also about yourself.

Big Talk aims to address the following societal needs:

1. **Build belonging and connection in communities.** Big Talk conversations, tools, and programs foster a more profound sense of connection and belonging for community members.

2. **Foster empathy and curiosity across cultures.** Big Talk's approach to conversation encourages individuals to relate to each other and share their

life stories to celebrate humanity, bridge divides, and foster empathy.

3. **Fight loneliness and isolation to improve mental and social health.** Big Talk helps us share our most vulnerable selves to form authentic, sustainable relationships and fight loneliness.
4. **Deepen friendships and strengthen relationships.** Big Talk questions help individuals go beyond small talk, fostering deeper, more meaningful connections with friends, family, colleagues, and partners.

How to Read This Book

To get the most out of this book, I recommend you:

1. **Set an intention.** Take a moment to reflect. Why are you reading this book? Is it to deepen existing relationships, introduce Big Talk to your workplace or community, make new friends, become a better listener, navigate social anxiety, strengthen your connections with family members, or bring more depth to dating and romantic connections? Clarifying your purpose will help guide your approach and make the experience more meaningful.

2. **Read each section in order.** Feel free to skim through the book first, highlighting or underlining parts that resonate with you. Then, try taking it slow: Read one chapter per week, treating the book as a meaningful personal journey or course.

3. **Practice the Big Talk conversation questions.** Apply them with others and take on the challenges at the end of each chapter. Refer back to sections when facing situations that could benefit from Big Talk.

4. **Use the Big Talk questions for reflection.** Answer them out loud or write them in a journal to contribute to your self-understanding and growth.

5. **Share your insights.** Talk through what you've learned with peers, friends, and family and invite them to join you in making Big Talk a part of your conversations.

6. **Be patient with yourself and others.** Remember that mastering Big Talk is an ongoing journey. It takes time, practice, and patience. Try not to rush the process or feel discouraged by setbacks.

7. **Notice the impact.** Pay attention to how your conversations evolve and how they influence your relationships. Notice how it feels to connect with others on a deeper level. Journal about your triumphs and experiences.

Remember, learning is an active process that requires attention and practice. The more you apply the principles in this book, the easier it will be to skip the small talk in everyday life. The first time I tried to make Big Talk, I felt awkward and struggled to keep the conversation going. Now, it flows more naturally than small talk!

1

Big Talk 101

Remember that everyone you meet is afraid of something, loves something, and has lost something.

—H. JACKSON BROWN, *THE COMPLETE LIFE'S LITTLE INSTRUCTION BOOK*

My approach to teaching Big Talk is built more on personal encounters than academic theories. In fact, the word *educator* comes from the Latin word *educare*, which means "to bring out what is within." In that spirit, I'm here with you—not as an instructor, but as a guide and fellow human—helping to draw out what's already within you!

Thousands of conversations have shaped the ideas and lessons in this book. I've discovered that genuine connection can happen anywhere, with anyone. By sharing stories, reflections, and moments that have moved me, I hope to help you open a path toward deeper connection.

Do it now.

On a sunlit walk with a friend in Venice Beach, an English couple stopped to ask me for directions. We struck up a conversation and moved past small talk, diving into Big Talk.

> ***Big Talk:*** *What is a brave choice you're glad you made?*
>
> ***English woman:*** *Some years ago, I was promoted to the job I had been trying to get for five years. Sadly, at that time, my youngest sister was diagnosed with terminal cancer. I remember when we were little kids, we used to play together with our teddy bears.*
>
> *I decided to give up the job to look after her. We spent her last few weeks together.*
>
> *I'm glad I made that decision, which I think is part of my "Do it now" philosophy. Because she was just forty-nine when she died. Literally, on her deathbed, she listed all the things she hadn't done. Because at forty-nine, you haven't done everything you wanted to do. So, if you've got a bucket list, do it; do it now. Don't wait. Too many people put things off, and you never know what's around the corner. So, take advantage of being alive today, and don't put things off. Do it now.*

This conversation reminded me what matters most in life: being there with the people you love and following your heart.

As Albert Einstein said, "Everything should be made as simple as possible, but not simpler."[1] This book aims to simplify the process of making meaningful connections while still honoring their significance.

Before we dive deep, we'll start with the basics. Think of this chapter as a primer or tool kit—a collection of ideas and practical tips to help you build a strong foundation for making Big Talk. In the chapters ahead, we'll explore the nuances, concepts, and deeper stories that transform Big Talk from conversation into connection.

Everyone has the ability—and the right—to build deeper connections. You don't need to be an extrovert or a community leader, in therapy, or studying communications. You just need to be open to talking and listening to people.

Even if some people seem unapproachable or distant, remember that they, too, like everyone else, may silently carry a fond memory, ceaseless worry, or life dream.

Sometimes, I like to think of connection as a series of simple "equations" that capture the essence of meaningful interactions:

- Curiosity + Empathy = A Big Talk Conversation
- A Shared Experience + Openness to Others = A New Relationship
- Shared Celebrations and Struggles + Collaboration = Community Building

These equations can help us frame social interactions to foster connection. Whether starting a conversation or strengthening a relationship, the key ingredients are always curiosity, openness, sharing, and empathy.

Before we get into the mechanics of making Big Talk, let's talk about what Big Talk actually is (and isn't).

Big Talk is:

- A communication approach for moving past small talk to ask deeper, more substantive questions and to make more meaningful life connections with just about anybody.
- A pathway to strengthening interpersonal relationships and building friendships.
- A storytelling tool to foster curiosity and empathy.
- A community-building tool to enhance belonging.
- An activity for self-reflection.

Big Talk is not:

- An excuse to step across people's boundaries and/or dive into political opinions.
- A therapy session or a substitute for professional mental health support.
- A platform for dominating conversations or proving a point.
- A one-size-fits-all approach—every conversation should adapt to the comfort and context of the people involved.
- A quick fix for building deep relationships, which takes time and genuine effort.

Remember that Big Talk doesn't always involve long, philosophical conversations, nor does it force others into uncomfortable, deep discussions. The goal is to make room for connection without pressure and allow exchanges to happen naturally.

So you may be wondering, how does one make Big Talk? Big Talk begins with the art of asking questions. There are three simple guidelines for what makes a question "Big Talk."

Big Talk questions are:

1. **Open-ended:** They invite more than a factual or "yes or no" response.
2. **Universal:** Any human being can answer them, no matter who they are or what they do. Big Talk conversations connect rather than divide.
3. **Story-eliciting:** Everyone would have a unique answer to the question, which invites people to share personal life experiences rather than discuss the outside world (e.g., the news or politics).

For example:

Question	Open-ended	Universal	Story-eliciting
Who are you voting for?	No	No	Maybe
What's the weather like today?	No	Yes	No
What was your childhood dream, and how has your path evolved since then?	Yes	Yes	Yes

If asking a profound question feels awkward to you, gradually move from small talk to Big Talk. If you still feel strange about it, tell the person that you are reading a book called *Big Talk* and were prompted to ask someone a more meaningful question beyond small talk this week. You might be surprised to learn more about someone in five minutes of Big Talk than you had in the weeks or months of other small talk conversations.

Conversation Openers: From Open-Ended Small Talk to Big Talk

When meeting someone new for the first time, there is an art to transitioning from small talk to Big Talk. Try offering a light and friendly opener, which makes the receiving person more likely to accept your transition.

Here are some great conversation starters that strike a balance between being approachable and inviting deeper conversation:

1. "Hi! I love [compliment]. Where did you discover it? / How did you come to be that way? / What influences your taste?"

   → *Genuine and specific compliments are a great way to start conversations. They allow a person to share something more personal.*

2. "Hello! I'm looking for [place or item]. Do you know where I can find it / how to get there? How did you come to be so knowledgeable about [X]?"

   → *Asking for help is a natural way to start a conversation. It can lead to some shared experiences or helpful tips. The key is to thank them and then ask follow-up questions about their knowledge.*

3. "I've noticed [something about the environment]—Do you see it too? What do you think?"

   → *Commenting on the environment—whether music, architecture, a local event, art, or something else—is a spontaneous and casual way to invite the other person to share an experience or observation with you.*

4. "Are you local? I'm interested in learning more about [X]." Or "Hi, I'm [your name]. I'm trying to get to know people and the area around here. What do you love about this neighborhood? I'm grateful for recommendations!"

   → *If you're traveling or just moved to a new area, this is a natural way to engage with a local. People usually love giving advice, and this question invites them to share their personal experiences and tips. It can also make them feel knowledgeable and helpful.*

5. "I've been wondering about [X]. What do you think?"

   → *Asking for an opinion on something (avoid politics) that is a conversation starter (like something happening around you) is a great way to establish rapport.*

6. "This might sound random, but what's something you're really into right now?"

   → *Acknowledging randomness eliminates awkward questions. This question is open and curious, allowing the other person to express their current hobbies, interests, or projects.*

These openers are not too invasive, but they are engaging enough to invite a response that can naturally transition small talk to Big Talk.

Once you have established rapport with someone, you can move into Big Talk (we will cover more of that throughout this book). After asking a Big Talk question, remember to:

1. Practice active listening and ask follow-up questions to demonstrate your interest while digging deeper.
2. Be authentic and share vulnerabilities.
3. Show empathy and find a commonality (this could be a shared idea, passion, experience, struggle, or story).

Tips for Making Big Talk

- **Avoid superlatives:** Superlatives can pigeonhole people into giving simple answers. Instead of using phrases like "most" or "favorite," try using phrases like "one of the" or "some." For example, instead of asking, "What was your favorite part of the trip?" ask, "What are some memorable moments from the trip?"
- **Consider the past and future:** Ask questions that help you learn about someone's history or future aspirations. For example:
  - "Have you always wanted to do [X], or was there a turning point in your life?"
  - "What goals do you hope to achieve in the coming years?"
  - "What is your dream for the future?"
- **Avoid using technology as a crutch:** Instead of reaching for your phone when feeling socially awkward, smile and look around. Try walking around or connecting with someone else in the room.
- **Accept rejection:** Not everyone will engage in Big Talk, and that's okay. Recognize when someone isn't comfortable with deeper conversation and move on. A conversation requires both participants to be willing to engage.
- **Know your environment:** Some environments are better for Big Talk than others. Great settings include road

trips, team-bonding events, dinner parties, and community meetings. Avoid making Big Talk in office spaces or meetings with rushed agendas, where the focus is on tasks rather than personal connection.

- **Ask to ask a question:** Sometimes the simplest gateway to making Big Talk is just asking, "Can I ask you a question?" Asking for permission first helps the other person feel more comfortable and in control. It also prepares them to expect something a little deeper or out of the ordinary.
- **Ask a person, not just the internet:** If you're curious about something, try asking a real person instead of immediately turning to the internet. It gives them a chance to share their perspective or knowledge—and gives you a chance to connect on a human level.
- **Ask "What's the story of . . . ?":** When you notice something unique about someone, turn your curiosity into connection by asking, "What's the story of . . . ?" For example: "What's the story of your tattoo?" or "What's the story of how you broke your leg?" Questions like these invite personal storytelling and often lead to meaningful conversations.

Network and Connect More Effectively with Big Talk

A friend of mine who is a rapper and producer told me he takes a stack of Big Talk Question Cards to music industry events. When he meets someone new, he invites them to draw a card and answer a question.

This simple approach helps steer conversations away from surface-level exchanges and makes him memorable. If carrying physical cards doesn't appeal to you, you can still reframe typical small talk questions into more substantive ones that create meaningful connections.

Alternative Ways to Ask "What Do You Do?"

The question "What do you do?" is often asked in social settings, but it usually results in a standard career-focused answer. To spark a deeper conversation, try asking:

- "What do you love to do?"
- "What does your world look like?"
- "How do you spend your days?"
- "What are you passionate about?"
- "What's your idea of a perfect day?"
- "What projects are you working on that excite you?"

More Small Talk vs. Big Talk Examples

Here's how you can transform small talk into Big Talk and turn typical topics into more meaningful conversations around personal experiences and emotions:

- From Weather to Values:
    - Small Talk: "It's so nice out!"
    - Big Talk: "How do you love to spend a beautiful day outside?"

- From Work to Passion:
  - Small Talk: "How's work?"
  - Big Talk: "What projects are you excited about working on right now?"
- From Hobbies to Growth:
  - Small Talk: "What are your hobbies?"
  - Big Talk: "What new activities are you excited to explore?"
- From Compliments to Meaning:
  - Small Talk: "Nice outfit!"
  - Big Talk: "What inspires your sense of style? Where do you love to shop that others might not know about?"
- From Family to Relationships:
  - Small Talk: "How's your family?"
  - Big Talk: "What recent memories have you made with your family?" / "What's a new memory you hope to create with your family soon?"
- From Current Events to Values:
  - Small Talk: "Did you hear about (current event)?"
  - Big Talk: "How do you feel about the direction we're moving in as a community?"

Creating Your Own Big Talk Questions

This book offers plenty of examples of Big Talk questions, but you'll soon be able to develop your own questions. Think about what you genuinely want to know. Is there something you're curious about or going through that could spark a conversation? Perhaps you're grieving and want to know how others cope with loss. Developing your own Big Talk questions based on universal human experiences can help you move past surface-level exchanges. Remember, your questions should be open-ended, meaningful, and universal. Instead of yes/no questions, ask things that open the door to deeper reflection. For example, if you're going through a period of transformation, ask, "What's something you've changed your perspective on recently, and why?"

Practice Makes Perfect!

Big Talk takes practice. It's a skill that grows over time. With every conversation, you'll improve at turning small talk into a chance to truly understand and connect with others. The more you practice, the more fulfilling your interactions will become.

Safety First

When engaging in Big Talk or any activity, prioritize physical and emotional safety for yourself and others. Trust your gut—if something feels off, don't proceed.

Emotional Safety Tips

- **Respect boundaries:** Let people decline questions without judgment.
- **Show empathy:** Respond kindly to vulnerable stories. I often say, "Thank you for sharing."
- **Be patient:** Allow time for processing. I say things like "Take your time" or "We can skip this question if you prefer not to answer."

Physical Safety Tips

- **Choose safe spaces:** I prefer parks, cafés, community centers, or tourist zones, which are well-lit and have other people around.
- **Don't go alone:** I sometimes bring my husband or a friend on walks to feel safer when talking to strangers.
- **Stick to familiar places:** Pick locations you know and can navigate easily.
- **Stay prepared:** Secure your phone, keys, and wallet, bring water, and know where restrooms are.
- **Be mindful of your body language:** Sometimes, I offer a handshake and other times, I keep more distance.

If Someone Is in Crisis

- **Recognize distress:** Look for silence, agitation, or someone seeming overwhelmed. Stay calm and compassionate.

- **Offer support:** Ask how they're feeling and what might help. Sometimes, stepping outside for fresh air or deep breathing can make a difference.
- **Seek help if needed:** If someone mentions self-harm, ask directly and call 911 if there's immediate danger. Otherwise, gently suggest they talk to a counselor or trusted confidante. For more resources, visit "Crisis Hotlines and Resources," American Psychological Association, apa.org/topics/crisis-hotlines.

A Thought to Keep in Mind

Big Talk is about creating meaningful conversations and deeper connections, but it's important to remember it's not a substitute for professional mental health support. While conversations can be powerful, they can't replace therapy, counseling, or medical care for mental health challenges, substance abuse, debilitating grief, trauma, or other serious personal struggles. Big Talk is meant to enrich your life and foster understanding, but sometimes, it's about knowing when to seek professional guidance. By prioritizing emotional and physical safety, you can build a strong foundation for impactful conversations while being mindful of when to encourage the right support.

As you move through the following pages, you'll learn how to deepen your conversations and boost your confidence in making Big Talk part of your everyday life.

Summary

Big Talk questions are open-ended, universal, and story-eliciting. After asking a question, practice active listening, be vulnerable, and find commonalities to build empathy.

CHALLENGE: START PRACTICING BIG TALK

1. **Turn small talk into Big Talk.** Next time you engage in small talk, try turning your questions into opportunities for deeper conversation. For example, after asking, "How are you doing?" or "What do you do?" follow up with questions like "What's been on your mind lately?" or "What's your dream?"
2. **Ask follow-up questions.** Dig deeper by asking questions like "What's the story behind that?" or "Why does that matter to you?"
3. **Take a risk.** Share something deeper about yourself after they answer, creating a more vulnerable exchange.
4. **Introduce a Big Talk question.** Start your next group dinner, one-on-one meeting, or community gathering with a question like "What is something you're excited to share with the group?" or "What's a lesson you've learned recently?"

SELF-REFLECTION QUESTIONS

Take on an extra challenge by journaling your responses to these Big Talk questions (see the Big Talk Questions Bank at the end of the book for more). Try them out as morning, afternoon, or evening reflection exercises—whatever works best for you. You can also find a reflection partner to converse with. Sometimes, it helps to go for a walk!

1. What is something you want to do more of when you begin to connect with others? What is something you want to do less of?
2. What are five things you want to do before you die? Are you living your life in line with these goals and dreams?
3. Are there people you haven't been in touch with in a long time who you want to reach out to? How would you like to nurture and evolve your relationship with them?

2

Be More Approachable

Too often we underestimate the power of a smile, a kind word, a listening ear, an honest compliment, or the smallest act of caring, all of which have the potential to turn a life around.

— LEO F. BUSCAGLIA, *LOVE*

When I was five, I visited China for the first time. My grandparents lived in Shanghai, and I was captivated by the large city with entirely new people. While on a morning walk with my grandfather, he said to me, eyes sparkling, "Did you know that I am friends with everyone in the entire world?!"

My five-year-old self was skeptical. He said, "I'll prove it to you." We strolled and meandered through the neighborhood. Everywhere we went, he stopped, smiled, and said hi to each stranger we encountered, sparking a friendly conversation with them. He seemed to know the dogs too! After that, I believed that he was indeed friends with everyone in the world. He was one of the most approachable people I have known. In his red sweater, I likened him to Mister Rogers.

Being approachable starts with being aware of how others perceive us. For others to feel safe sharing personal stories with us, they must see us as friendly and trustworthy. Unknowingly, some of us come across as distant or stone-faced because we are shy or anxious. We might crave deeper connections without knowing how to initiate or express a receptiveness to them. We may see someone we'd be interested in talking to and play out an imaginary encounter with them in our minds, but then walk right on by with an averted gaze and never speak to them.

How would they ever know we wanted to talk to them if we can't even look them in the eye? When we position ourselves as more approachable, the potential connections that may unfold are limitless.

Make sure you spread the aloha!

I've visited Hawaii many times. The *'āina* (land) and the people who care for it hold a special place in my heart. During one visit, my mom and I went on an Earth Day waterfall hike. At the entrance, a Hawaiian man named Keoki stood with a warm smile, offering advice to visitors on how to honor the land. While most people passed by, I stopped to talk to him.

> ***Big Talk:*** *What beautiful natural sights have you seen?*
>
> ***Keoki:*** *When I was up at the Haleakalā volcano in Maui, all I could see were the volcano and the clouds surrounding us. It was a very feel-good moment be-*

cause I lost my grandmother last year. So it was pretty hard for me to do anything up until then. But I got out there, traveled, got to experience it, and took her with me in spirit. She always told me all the time, every place I went hiking and sent her photos—she always felt like she was with me looking through my eyes.

***Big Talk:** If you could share a message with the world, what would it be?*

***Keoki:** Be involved. Everybody always asks me, "What is it to be Hawaiian?" Being Hawaiian means being with the land, the ʻāina, planting things, maintaining them, and pulling weeds. That is what being Hawaiian means, and you should make sure you spread the aloha!*

A few people from Hawaii told me they appreciated an outsider's willingness to share the aloha and remind people of what matters—honoring the land. I appreciated Keoki's approachable demeanor, which allowed me (and many others) to learn from him!

Being approachable is the first characteristic necessary for starting a Big Talk conversation. Try these simple strategies to be more approachable and invite more opportunities for Big Talk!

15 Strategies for Becoming More Approachable for Meaningful Conversations

1. Smile and make eye contact. Look people directly in the eye with a sincere smile, and you'll be surprised by the conversations and interactions your warmth will invite! Eckhart Tolle said, "When you smile at a stranger, there is already a minute outflow of energy. You become a giver."[1] An authentic smile signifies kindness and goodwill, making people feel comfortable. This small gesture builds trust and opens the door to connection.

2. Ask for their name, then repeat it back to them. When you meet someone new, immediately ask for their name. Then repeat it back to them and introduce yourself. Dale Carnegie wrote, "A person's name is to him or her the sweetest and most important sound in any language."[2] People love to hear the sound of their names—it's the closest connection to their identity, helping them feel seen and heard. By repeating a name back to a stranger, you are more likely to remember it (and they get the added serotonin boost of hearing their name again).

3. Use your "friendly voice." We all have different voices for different occasions, i.e., our phone voice, our meeting voice, the voice we use when talking to a cute animal. My voice for Big Talk conversations is optimistic, friendly, easygoing, and playful. It's the kind of voice that says, "I'm a positive person who is interested in you and what you have to share."

4. Practice mirroring. Have you ever noticed how close friends or couples laugh the same way or pick up each other's habits? Sometimes, people even seem to resemble their dogs! They are mirroring each other.

Mirroring involves subtly reflecting someone's behaviors, tone, pace, and gestures to build trust and rapport. The unconscious act of mirroring will help people feel more connected and comfortable with you.

5. Stop rushing around. Psychologist Mary Pipher wrote, "The two most radical things you can do in America are to slow down, and to talk to each other."[3] If you look busy or rushed, people are unlikely to approach you. Instead, try to slow down, bring awareness to your surroundings, and notice the people around you. The person you often rush past on your way to work could become a close neighbor or friend.

I love the quote by Yoko Ono: "Speeding up is always the wrong thing to do. Give yourself a chance to go by the rhythm of your own heart."[4] It reminds us to trust our own pace and follow our most natural whims. Then, we can attract people who match our values and energy.

6. Visit third spaces. "Third spaces" are environments outside of home and work where people gather and connect to enjoy themselves. You're more likely to meet friendly people in places of leisure where people are unrushed and engaged in relaxing activities. Spaces that naturally foster connection include parks, beaches, tourist hot spots, festivals, community events, interest groups, classes, cafés, libraries, and celebrations. In these places, people are more likely to be happy and relaxed. Happy people are more approachable because their worries are cast aside. I chose to film the first Big Talk video at a beach, park, outdoor shopping center, and museum for this reason. Relaxed environments set the stage for genuine interactions.

7. Avoid microflights from intimacy. Microflights are subtle actions that create distance between people.[5] You might not even know you're doing them. By reducing these tendencies, you can make space for deeper conversations.

Some examples of microflights from intimacy:

- Checking your phone or computer during a heartfelt conversation
- Avoiding eye contact with people
- Changing the subject when someone asks a more engaging or personal question
- Using humor to deflect from more serious conversations
- Rushing through conversations

Microflights can originate from fears of vulnerability, but by noticing them, you can cultivate more open connections with others!

8. Let others lead with approachability. Someone once sent me a photo of a rideshare driver who kept a jar of Big Talk questions in his car. It was his way of signaling he was approachable and inviting connection without forcing it. This approach respects people's boundaries while creating space for engagement.

9. Participate in public activities that inspire connection. Engaging in unique activities can make you more approachable and spark curiosity in others. Whether it's bird-watching, playing the ukulele outdoors, testing out a new camera or gadget, playing sports, or painting your view outside, doing something interesting gives others a natural conversation starter. In 2024, I set up a Big Talk table at various community festivals, from a mental health fair to a summer-solstice beach party. People from all walks of life approached me and shared their stories—from triumphs in cancer recovery to road trip adventures. Participating in something public and meaningful in the community opened the door for people to approach me and connect.

10. Be aware of how others perceive you. While Big Talk celebrates authenticity, it's essential to be mindful of how our physical presence can influence a conversation. For example, if you try to initiate Big Talk with a young woman, she might feel cautious, especially in unfamiliar situations. If you are a young adult just starting in the professional world and trying to make Big Talk with an older wealthy person, they might think you want something from them and be more guarded.

Awareness of body language allows you to make others feel more at ease while remaining genuine. It is essential not to be intrusive when making yourself approachable for Big Talk. Not everyone wants to chat, and that's okay! A key element to being approachable is to be aware of your surroundings and know when to initiate interactions. If someone appears preoccupied, it may not be the best time to make contact. You can only do so much, and that's okay! This awareness will foster more empathy toward others' needs.

11. Drop your ego. Practice the art of clearing. Clear your mind of preoccupations before engaging with others. Journaling, meditating, or venting to a trusted friend can help free your mental space. When your energy is open and present, others will pick up on this and feel more drawn to you.

12. Don't be afraid to stand out with a conversation starter. Wear something unusual, have something unique on your desk, or do something that some might consider a little "out there." People will be drawn to you!

For example, every morning, I'd see the same man sitting at a table outside Starbucks in a sharp suit with a single flower tucked into his lapel. He sat there proudly, as if it were his office, sipping his coffee. One day, I finally walked up and said, "I love your suit—and that flower! It's such a great touch." He smiled, thanked me, introduced himself as Jonnie, and we ended up talking for half an hour. He told me that in life, it's important to "find something to love and not let anything get you too down." He shared stories about overcoming addiction after too many "close calls," surviving leukemia, and now living for his five grandchildren. He said he wore the suit because he was proud to be alive. "Realize how lucky you are to have your life," he said, "and keep going forward with it in a positive way."

It was a heartfelt conversation outside a Starbucks on what could have been an ordinary morning. His suit with that single flower—a simple and unique outfit—was Jonnie's invitation. If he hadn't worn it, I might not have had the courage to say hello. So don't be afraid to stand out. You never know who might be waiting for a reason to connect.

13. Share your art and creativity with the world. One powerful way to gain a window into someone's soul—and create a pathway to Big Talk—is by sharing each other's art and music. I've often written someone off as conventional only to later stumble upon their social media and discover they play in a band or create intricate collages. Suddenly, I see a whole new dimension of who they are. Their art becomes a doorway to deeper understanding and a richer conversation.

That's why whenever I visit someone's home for the first time, I always notice the art on their walls and the books on their shelves. These small details often tell the biggest stories.

So don't be afraid to share your creativity publicly. Art is one of the most personal reflections of our identity. Every individual is an artist, whether they believe it or not. Sharing your art with the public can invite people into your inner world and prompt Big Talk conversations.

For example, one afternoon, I was walking along the beach and spied something so unique and beautiful that I had to stop. A man was sculpting a sandcastle. He covered it in an array of fresh flowers. Brilliant purple, pink, orange, and white flowers dotted the towers and hills of the castle. I asked him why he made these flower sandcastles. He told me that he was going through a dark time at one point and didn't know if it was worth being here anymore. But these sandcastles were his simple act of sharing beauty and worth with the world.

I was stunned by the depth of his words and the intent behind his art. He brought beauty and hope into the world, and we made a sincere connection because I could see, hear, and feel it all at once. If I had just seen him walking down the street, I wouldn't have had as much reason to interact with him.

Think about the art you have inside you. Do you like to paint, build, decorate cakes, garden, or play music? Now, think about how to publicly share your art and connect with others who will appreciate it.

In his book, *Show Your Work!*, author Austin Kleon puts it simply: "Make stuff you love and talk about stuff you love and you'll attract people who love that kind of stuff. It's that simple."[6]

So, there you have it. Make something you love and then share it through conversation or demonstration. Sign up for an art walk, a maker fair, or a farmers' market, or busk outdoors. You'll attract conversation and like-minded people.

14. Watch for second encounters and trust the universe's timing. There have been moments when I noticed an intriguing stranger—perhaps it was how they carried themselves, what they were doing, or how they dressed. I would watch them intently, feeling an urge to say hello, but often, I felt too shy and let them walk away. On a few occasions, I saw these individuals a second time and took it as a sign from the universe that we were destined to connect.

For example, I noticed an older woman in a glamorous dress being honored at a mental health gala. While presenting a Big Talk workshop to city officials a few months later, I spotted her again. I gathered my courage, walked up to her, and mentioned that I recognized her from the gala. We ended up having a meaningful conversation, during which I learned that both her parents had committed suicide, motivating her lifelong commitment to mental health advocacy.

Another memorable encounter occurred when I saw a man announcing native Hawaiian musicians at Duke's Restaurant in Waikiki. His charisma and presence were captivating. I could tell he was a local legend. I wanted to say hello and compliment him, but I hesitated and lost my chance. A year later, I returned to Hawaii, and on my last day, I saw that same man announcing a hula show by the beach. I watched the entire performance, and afterward, I approached him and asked him about his journey in entertainment. His name was Kimo, and we had a delightful conversation! It made my trip to Hawaii even more memorable to connect with a cultural steward.

Seeing someone a second time can feel like a little nudge from the universe that our paths are meant to cross, even if we don't quite understand why yet. These moments remind us that every encounter has the potential to be something special. So the next time you see someone twice, maybe it's worth saying hello; you never know where that connection might lead!

15. Declutter your life to become calmer and ground yourself. People can sense nervous energy. To be approachable and present for others, you must first find calm within yourself. Practice these techniques to ground and center yourself.

- **Try box breathing.** Inhale for four counts, hold for four, and exhale for four. Techniques like this help you radiate calmness, which is inherently inviting.
- **Connect with the earth.** Grounding practices like walking barefoot on grass or walking outdoors can help center you.
- **Declutter your life.** People sense when you're overwhelmed or distracted. To be genuinely approachable, make space for connection by decluttering.
    - **Say no.** Politely decline commitments that drain you.
    - **Prioritize.** Focus on what brings you joy and remove what doesn't.
    - **Declutter your space and schedule.** Create room for relaxation and meaningful interactions.
    - **Simplify digitally.** Unsubscribe, unfollow, and limit social media distractions.

The Coconut Girl

When I told a friend I was writing a chapter about being more approachable, he said, "That reminds me of the Coconut Girl!" In San Francisco, a woman conducted an experiment where she first carried a cup of coffee around on her walks through the city, then swapped it for a coconut. To her surprise, people were far more likely to approach her when she had the coconut. Something about the coconut made her appear more friendly.

A few months later, while at a farmers' market, I bought a coconut and sat down with a friend on a shady bench to relax. Soon after, a man on a bike stopped and asked if he could take our photo for his community project. We agreed, and he took a Polaroid of us.

A few months after that, at an art crawl in the Venice Canals, someone approached me and asked, "Are you the coconut girl?" He pulled out a stack of Polaroids and showed me the photo he had taken of us at the farmers' market. I thought, *How poetic!* Maybe there's something to this coconut theory of approachability after all.

Now, I'm not saying you should carry a coconut everywhere, but there's wisdom in having something about you that sparks playfulness and invites connection. Perhaps the coconut symbolizes the laid-back, friendly energy of island life. Similarly, you could carry a unique accessory, a friendly pet, a fun pin or hat, a book, a sketchbook, or even wear a T-shirt with an interesting design. Approachability is about being open to the possibilities around you, and sometimes the smallest acts can lead to unexpected, delightful connections.

Summary

Being approachable leads to opportunities to make more meaningful connections. You can become more approachable by smiling and making eye contact, asking people's names, slowing down, spending time in places where others are content, making yourself available to be approached, engaging in interesting activities that others can ask you about, and letting go of your ego. It is crucial to be approachable without intruding on others' time, space, and energy.

CHALLENGE: NEXT TIME YOU'RE OUT, AVOID TECHNOLOGY AND SMILE AT PEOPLE INSTEAD

For the next week, avoid looking at your phone whenever you are out and about and around other people. Resist the urge to pull it out when you feel bored or uncomfortable. Ignore notifications and vibrations—it can wait. Just keep it in your pocket, look up, and dare to smile at passersby. If you can, find something genuinely kind to express to someone and watch them light up. You might be surprised by how much better you feel and what kinds of conversations you can start!

BIG TALK CONVERSATION STARTERS FOR APPROACHABILITY

1. I love that you're doing ____. How did you get started? (*Compliment them.*)
2. What are you looking forward to? / What's your next adventure?

3. Where are you from? What would be your ideal day or weekend there?
4. What has been the best part of your week so far?
5. What do you like to do for fun when you are not working?
6. What is something you have always wanted to try?
7. What is a common misconception people have about you, or, What is a fun fact that people might not know immediately?

Remember to be genuine, ask follow-up questions, and adjust your questions based on the context of the situation or the person you are speaking with.

SELF-REFLECTION QUESTIONS: HOW APPROACHABLE ARE YOU?

1. What kind of first impression have you been told you give to others? Is this how you want to be perceived? If not, what can you do to change it?
2. What steps can you take to become more approachable to others?
3. Which types of people do you want to meet more of, and what kinds of new interactions do you crave? Where can you go, and what can you do to put yourself in a position to create these interactions?

3

Practice Curiosity

The greatest problem with communication is we don't listen to understand. We listen to reply. When we listen with curiosity, we don't listen with the intent to reply. We listen for what's behind the words.

—ROY T. BENNETT, *THE LIGHT IN THE HEART*

The writer Ralph B. Smith once observed that children ask about 125 questions per day, while adults ask about six.[1] So, as we grow up, we lose 119 questions from our daily curiosity quota.

At what point do we lose our innate curiosity and candor to say what's on our minds? I once heard something a six-year-old said: "Grown-ups are weird because when you ask them, 'How are you?' they always say 'good,' even when they're not good!"

The truth is, everyone is going through or thinking about something you might not expect—and has a story worth sharing. You can't see it on the surface and won't discover it through small talk. Make space in your life for curiosity to flourish. Allow time to look up at the stars, search for treasures along a seashore, meander along a town's main street, or schedule a visit to see old teachers and friends. Time and space are rare to come by, but they are sacred and essential for cultivating curiosity.

Perfection is pure fiction, and progress is perfection.

A woman in my neighborhood reached out and suggested that I make Big Talk with her friend Bill, a therapist and deep thinker. Intrigued, I arranged to meet him at the Palisades Bluffs overlooking the Pacific Coast Highway. He wore a Hawaiian shirt, a rock star–style hoop earring in his right ear, and had dancing blue eyes. What followed was one of the more profound Big Talk conversations I've had.

> ***Big Talk:** Have you ever loved and lost someone?*
>
> ***Bill:** Yes, I have. I had a deep relationship for twenty-five years. It was like a soulmate friendship—through thick and thin, we always had each other's backs. I was in and out of the hospital for four years, and she passed away four years ago. I miss her every single day.*
>
> ***Big Talk:** What were your favorite memories with her?*
>
> ***Bill:** I used to ride a motorcycle, and one time we were in Big Sur. She had always dreamed of riding a motorcycle across one of those iconic bridges. She was on the back of my bike, and as we crossed, she started crying.*
>
> ***Big Talk:** What's a dream you have let go of?*

__Bill:__ That's a great question. Being thirty years old? (laughs) I've let go of having impossibly high expectations. I've realized that perfection is pure fiction, and progress is perfection. Accept what is. Be human and divine.

__Big Talk:__ What's your next adventure in life?

__Bill:__ I hope to meet my soulmate—a kindred spirit—and take her in my converted van up the western coast. We'd visit the national parks here and in Canada. That would be a dream come true.

As our conversation ended, Bill offered:

"One of the greatest questions is 'What makes you feel loved?' For me, it's when people ask me questions and show curiosity. I'm very enamored that you do this. I think it's a great service. You are doing holy work."

Bill's gratitude for curiosity reminded me of how vital it is to make others feel seen and that progress, not perfection, is the goal. Through Big Talk, I've discovered that when we take the time to ask thoughtful questions and listen, we perform a sacred act of making others feel seen, heard, and valued.

When I lead Big Talk workshops, one of the first questions I encourage people to ask is "What have you been curious about lately?"

This question gets to the crux of what people are thinking and helps us sidestep mundane small talk.

What Is Curiosity?

In the context of Big Talk, curiosity is:

- Building deeper connections by asking meaningful, fascinating, and thought-provoking questions.
- Self-reflecting on your interests, motivations, and actions as you learn and grow.
- Exploring new ideas and experiences, fueling a desire to discover the world and the people around you (making you more interesting!).
- Stepping outside your comfort zone and challenging assumptions, fostering creativity and personal growth.

Skipping small talk to practice curiosity can help us discover more about others and ourselves, form deeper connections, develop creative and innovative ideas, and become more engaged listeners.

The Case for Curiosity

It feels more natural to ask thoughtful, even provocative and unusual questions when you're genuinely curious about someone. Curiosity eases awkwardness and replaces hesitation with openness and candor—and in Big Talk, that can lead to powerful, meaningful connections.

It's impossible to imagine creativity or invention without curiosity. Many great historical, creative, and scientific discoveries began with someone determined to answer a big question. In the same way, we can use curiosity in Big Talk conversations to make significant discoveries about others and ourselves—discoveries that can lead to authentic and even surprising connections!

But to be an effective, curious question-asker, we must also be great listeners. Greek philosopher Epictetus stated, "We have two ears and one mouth, so that we can listen twice as much as we speak."[2]

When I lead Big Talk workshops, I ask questions and encourage others to share their stories. At the end, people often tell me I was the best speaker they ever had. Ironically, I don't speak much at all. Instead, I demonstrate curiosity by inviting participants to open up and talk out loud, making them feel seen and heard. In turn, this is what wins their hearts and minds!

How to Practice Curiosity

Sometimes you meet someone who seems like they have a thousand stories to tell. If curiosity strikes, don't hesitate. Embrace it and ask them a question.

When I see someone intriguing walking down the street, I can't help but wonder about them. Who are they? What's a typical day in their life? What are their passions, fears, and dreams? Curiosity isn't just an impulse—it's a practice. Rather than judging someone from the outside, try to dive deeper and question their interior life. I am always silently making up questions. For example:

- Why do they carry that forlorn/aloof/enthusiastic expression on their face?
- What do they secretly nerd out about?
- What is the hardest part of life right now for them?
- What makes them feel proud?
- How would they spend their time if they found out they had a limited time left on earth?

These musings fueled my curiosity and imagination, but I realized something over time: I could ask these questions. Now, through Big Talk, I do. When an elderly couple sitting on a bench smiled at me, I stopped and complimented their kind disposition and asked them about the secret to their happy and long marriage. When I saw a man living on the street reading by my window, I ventured outside and asked him what he was reading and searching for. To practice curiosity, lead a life of wonder and turn your observations into questions. For example:

- Take note of wonders in the world that spark your imagination. Turn them into questions to raise in your next conversation. If nothing has made you wonder lately, it might be time to turn off your devices, go outside for a walk, and look around. What piques your interest?
- Ask questions in order to uncover unexpected stories that go beyond the facts and help you build genuine relationships. For example, "What is a life story you seldom tell?"
- Listen intently and note what intrigues you about what they said or did. Then, dive deeper. Make the other person feel

learned or important by encouraging them in their knowledge. Say something like "It's so cool that you experienced [X]. I would love to learn more about how [X] led you to [Y]."

Give More Intriguing Answers to Pique Others' Curiosity About You

Curiosity isn't just about others—it's also about how we present ourselves. When someone asks, "What do you do?" it's tempting to stick to a basic job title. But consider how much richer the conversation could be if you offered a more intriguing answer.

Here are some ways I've answered this question instead of saying, "I'm a journalist" or "I'm an entrepreneur":

- "I run a movement called Big Talk where I skip small talk with strangers and ask them profound life questions."
- "I travel the world making videos, asking strangers meaningful questions for a living. I also love to surf, practice martial arts, and paint."

By sharing something more descriptive, personal, or unexpected, you invite curiosity and set the stage for a deeper conversation.

Fill Your Well

If you feel drained or uninspired lately, it's time to refill your well of curiosity. Read, travel, talk to people, experience culture, and look outward. What fascinates you lately? What sparks your sense of wonder? Filling your life with curiosity makes you more engaging and better equipped to connect with others.

One way to recharge is by seeking experiences that inspire awe. Awe improves mental health and reignites our love for the world and its people. Psychologist Dacher Keltner identifies eight wonders of life that evoke awe:

1. **Moral beauty:** Witnessing acts of virtue and kindness, especially in ordinary people doing extraordinary things.
2. **Collective effervescence:** Feeling connected in large gatherings like concerts, sporting events, or rallies.
3. **Nature:** Experiencing the majesty of the natural world.
4. **Music:** Being moved by melodies and rhythms, whether by listening or performing.
5. **Visual design:** Marveling at beautiful architecture, well-designed objects, or art.
6. **Spiritual experiences:** Feeling connected to something greater.
7. **Stories of life and death:** Moments that make us reflect on existence and life's fragility.
8. **Epiphanies:** Sudden realizations or moments of clarity that shift our perspective.[3]

In 2025, after the Los Angeles fires, I witnessed strangers from all walks of life coming together to help one another. I often found myself driving around in tears, overwhelmed by emotion. The smallest moments could bring them on—seeing a sign that said "Hope," watching a volunteer hand a water bottle to an exhausted elderly person, or noticing families standing in front of their burned-down neighborhoods holding signs that read "Not for Sale." Later, I learned I was experiencing what psychologists call "tears of moral elevation"—the kind that come from feeling awe in response to humanity's goodness. To invite awe into your life, practice noticing with all five senses. Ground yourself in the present by asking:

- "What do I see, hear, or sense right now?"
- "What is intriguing or beautiful about this moment?"

Once your well is full, share your awe and curiosity with others. Ask questions that uncover hidden fascinations:

- "What inspires you most these days?"
- "What moves you to tears of moral elevation?"
- "What are you reading, listening to, or watching lately?"
- "What's a mystery or problem that has always intrigued you?"
- "If you could spend a year learning about one thing, what would it be?"
- "What did you love exploring as a child that still excites you today?"

Go on a Curiosity Quest

Whether discovering answers to your family's history in a remote village of your ancestors, hunting for the best hole-in-the-wall restaurants in your hometown, or searching for secret waterfalls and swimming holes on a coastal road trip—quests are exciting ways to build bonds. For parents and kids, quests can be a fun and meaningful way to connect. I remember going on "rock walks" along the seashore with my dad when I was a kid. Now, I'm planning a quest to discover animal sanctuaries around the world, since my dream is to one day have one of my own. Go on a quest with your community, someone you love, or a friend you want to strengthen bonds with. Whether you're solving a mystery or exploring a new place, the journey of your curiosity quest is the destination.

How to Slow Down Time

In 2024, I decided to surf on a windy day at a secluded spot in the southeast of Oahu, Hawaii. Not long after paddling out, I caught a wave, hit a bump, and flew off my surfboard. A powerful gust of wind lifted the board, and the rail slammed into my forehead, splitting it open.

Time began to slow down. I remember every moment that followed: paddling frantically toward a narrow keyhole in the shoreline, a kind Hawaiian woman wrapping a towel around my head to stop the bleeding as she spoke to me about the dangers and beauties of the natural world, the drive to the ER, the faces and discussions of the people in the waiting room, the calm conversation with the doctor about his upcoming engagement as he stitched my face, and the delicious meal I savored that night, overwhelmed with joy and gratitude to be alive and safe.

That was the most memorable afternoon of my trip. Despite the injury and lingering scar on my face, I cherish the memory more than any other moment from my vacation.

Have you ever noticed how time seems to stretch and elongate during exhilarating or new experiences, yet flies by in our daily routines? That's because novel environments and situations activate areas of the brain associated with memory and presence. People who engage in new activities and experiences report time feeling slower and richer.[4]

To "slow down" time, embrace new experiences and invite others to join you. Ask:

- What can I do today that's new or meaningful?
- Who can I share this with to make it even more special?
- What excites me or gets my adrenaline pumping?

Curiosity Opens Doors

A friend of mine has a mantra: "Let them say no." This mantra reminds us that we often say no to ourselves before anyone else has the chance.

One day, we were walking on one of my favorite streets in the neighborhood when a painting through a window caught my eye. I was mesmerized by swirls of pastel greens, blues, whites, peaches, and pinks. It reminded me of a sunrise reflected on a shimmering pond.

I said, "Oh, I wish I knew who painted that!" My friend immediately replied, "Why don't we knock on the door and find out?"

I hesitated. "Knock on a stranger's door? Nobody does that anymore!" But she just smiled and said, "Let them say no."

So, we knocked. An older woman answered, and to my amazement, she led us downstairs to meet her husband—the painter of the masterpiece in the window! He showed us his studio of "unfinished works" and their backyard, a secret garden of koi ponds and lush plants. He told us he no longer exhibits his work, so we were lucky to have an exclusive look at his breathtaking creations. That encounter showed me the power of bold curiosity. I'm grateful my friend nudged me to follow my wonder—and to knock on the door.

When we step outside our routines, whether by exploring a new world or making Big Talk with a stranger, we create memories that deepen our appreciation for life and each other. In your social interactions this week, question everything with wonder.

Even in the middle of your busy day—when your phone is calling your name, your to-do list won't stop growing, and someone on the subway is blasting their speaker so loudly you can't hear your own thoughts—curiosity is still there, waiting for you to notice something new. Curiosity can thrive in the chaos.

In a crowded café, you might overhear someone talking about something intriguing, look it up later, or bring it up in conversation with a friend. At a professional event full of small talk, you might ask someone what exciting goals they've been pursuing outside of work. In a ride-share in a new city, you might ask the driver what paths led them to this point. I've met ride-share drivers who are artists, parents, teachers, and even former neighbors.

Remember, it's not just the question you ask that matters; it's the curiosity to ask the question in the first place and then explore the answer that makes the most significant difference.

Summary

Curiosity leads to richer experiences, creativity, likability, awe, deeper connections, and becoming a more fascinating person. You can apply curiosity by leading a life of wonder, asking thoughtful, open-ended questions, and listening.

CHALLENGE: CURIOSITY SCAVENGER HUNT

The next chance you have time to explore your environment—whether traveling or at home—try out this scavenger hunt to practice being more curious. See how many of these tasks you can accomplish:

1. **Notice** something intriguing about a place, idea, or stranger and ask someone about it. Then, if they are receptive to you, continue the conversation and dive deeper to explore your curiosity.

2. **Visit** a community, cultural institution, museum, or small business you wouldn't usually visit. Ask the owner or tour guide/artist about their interests and how they became involved.

3. **Explore** a new area of town. Ask a local about the history and favorite spots that people might not

typically know about or think of. Find out what brought them to that area and what makes it feel like home to them.

4. **Strike up a conversation** with an older adult and soak in their wisdom. If you befriend them, invite them to share in tea or a meal.
5. **Reflect on your journey,** take a camera, sketchbook, or journal, and photograph, sketch, or write about the sights, sounds, and sensations.

CURIOUS BIG TALK QUESTIONS TO ASK OTHERS BEYOND "HOW ARE YOU?" AND "WHAT DO YOU DO?"

1. What have you been curious about lately?
2. What new habit do you want to form, and why?
3. What is something unexpected you recently tried and enjoyed?
4. If you could learn any new skill(s) this year, what would they be?
5. What are the most interesting things you have read, seen, listened to, or learned about lately?
6. What is something that most people do not know about you? What is the story behind that?

7. What is some of the best advice you have received lately? How does that advice relate to how you want to lead your life?
8. What does your world look like lately?

CURIOUS QUESTIONS TO ASK YOURSELF

1. If I could do a deep dive or make a documentary about any subject matter, what would it be?
2. Why do I do what I do daily? Am I pleased with this routine? If I could take a step back, would I change anything?
3. What would I do if I could not fail? What are the consequences if I fail, and how might I recover from them?
4. What are the unknowns in my life right now that I want to figure out? What are the unknowns in the world that I am curious about? How do I discover more about all of them?
5. What is a thought pattern I would like to change?

4

Set Intentions

It has been said that the "shortest distance between two points is an intention."

—RICHARD CARLSON, *DON'T SWEAT THE SMALL STUFF*

I once met a man from Australia named Seb. After the sudden loss of his childhood friend, he wrote a list of one hundred things he wanted to accomplish before he died. Since then, he has completed seventy-seven of them. He's helped a man in a wheelchair cross a race's finish line, visited a death-row inmate, and skydived completely naked. By setting the intention to create this list and pursuing it over the years, Seb has built a life filled with purpose and adventure!

Setting intentions isn't just for bucket lists. Municipal leaders set an agenda before a city council meeting so that the goals of the meeting are clear and people know how to prepare. So, why shouldn't we do the same for our personal lives to be more purposeful and well-prepared for upcoming interactions?

For example, when I was invited to several bachelorette parties in my twenties, I was a little anxious, having never been to one before. I confided in a friend, and she suggested, "Why don't you set a few intentions for the weekend?" I thought about it and set three intentions: 1) Make sure the bride feels loved and comfortable. 2) Take time to bond with each guest, getting to know them one-on-one. 3) Explore a new city and note what piques my joy and curiosity. With those intentions in mind, I instantly felt more at ease. Needless to say, I had a fantastic weekend and bonded with the other guests.

You could be lonely in a crowd. You could be lonely by yourself.

Sometimes, I leave my house intending to have a Big Talk conversation. It's a way of manifesting in which I think about who I'd like to meet and what I'd like to learn from them. At one point, I considered making a documentary about loneliness. I was at a park and saw a man sitting alone for a while, so I walked up to him to ask him about his life. He went by Joe.

> *Big Talk: Do you ever feel lonely?*
>
> *Joe: Who doesn't? You could be lonely in a crowd. You could be lonely by yourself. My journey has been both darkness and light. It's okay. It's okay to feel the hurt. And it's okay to feel all the things that keep us closed off or maybe make us want to close off. But it's not okay to stay there. It's accepting that these are challenges, that this is the world, and that people may not*

always be present. But we can help them. We can help ourselves. And we can open hearts by being willing to be someone who is more than just a passerby.

I never would have approached Joe if loneliness hadn't been on my mind. Instead, I met a kind and thoughtful man who echoed so many of my own thoughts. This reminded me of a quote from Thich Nhat Hanh, a Buddhist monk: "The intention of deep listening and loving speech is to restore communication, because once communication is restored, everything is possible."[1]

Time is the most valuable resource we can spend. Bronnie Ware, an Australian nurse who worked in palliative care, once recorded the top regrets of the dying. One common lament was "I wish I'd had the courage to express my feelings."[2] If this is true for most of us, why would we waste our time on superficial small talk? Why not just "express our feelings"? It takes real effort and intention to express oneself purposefully and emotively, even with our loved ones.

According to Ware, people who lead the most fulfilling lives are intentional about how they spend their time and with whom they build relationships. We can never turn back the hands of time, but we can choose to be present each day and set an intention for each moment and interaction we're blessed to experience.

In the context of making Big Talk, an intention is the purpose you bring to conversations. It means being mindful about why you are engaging in the conversation.

What does it take to be intentional?

- **Purpose:** Be purposeful with your time and have a clear reason for the interaction, whether it's to make a new and meaningful connection, learn something new from someone else's perspective, or share an important idea.
- **Discernment:** Be deliberate when initiating a conversation. Understand when and why you are talking (not just to fill space).
- **Authenticity:** Share your genuine and honest thoughts and feelings.
- **Presence:** Be fully present in the moment, engaging with the other person without distractions.
- **Empathy:** Consider the other person's feelings and perspectives. Approach the conversation with compassion.

Intentionality is not:

- Taking control of conversations, not allowing someone to get across their thoughts and ideas.
- Only talking to someone to obtain something from them.

Three Steps for Intentional Conversations

1. Self-Reflect

Self-reflect on whom you want to connect with and why. You may want to make new friendships or get to know your romantic partner or coworker better. Perhaps it's time to repair a relationship with a family member. Ask yourself self-reflective questions such as:

- Who would I reach out to because it has been too long or because it feels like it's the right time?
- Who is someone I want to know better? What do I want to know?
- What topics do I want to talk about more? What topics do I want to talk about less?

2. Make a Bid for Connection

Once you have set an intention about whom you want to connect with, it's time to make a bid. Drs. John and Julie Gottman of The Gottman Institute define a bid as an attempt to get attention, affection, and/or acceptance.[3] Before initiating a connection, ensure you have the proper physical, mental, and emotional presence.

Remember, being approachable for a conversation starts with body language (a smile, eye contact, a relaxed disposition). Clear your mind so that you're ready to talk to others. Then, dare to be the first to reach out warmly by exercising compassion and showing you care.

It often helps to have Big Talk prompts on hand that show you are passionate about connecting with them—positive questions that lead to productive and meaningful conversations. These conversations will allow you to connect more intentionally. You could use some of the following suggestions or develop your own.

- **Share curiosities.** "What have you been interested in exploring lately?"

- **Share updates.** "What was something memorable that happened to you since we last saw each other?"
- **Share accomplishments.** "What have you been proud of recently?"
- **Discuss common interests.** "What is something new we could try together next time we hang out?"

Making an intentional bid for connection can also mean setting aside time to make Big Talk a part of your life. A rapper from Chicago once messaged me about how he and his girlfriend used Big Talk:

> As part of our quality time, we'd answer one Big Talk Question Card together as a daily evening ritual and celebration of intimacy! As we continue to grow as individuals, we want to set intention by creating the space to keep connecting with ourselves and each other!

They have been together for ten years.

3. Practice WAIT—Why Am I Talking?

When having a Big Talk conversation, your responses should be as intentional as your questions. Ask yourself why you are responding; otherwise, you risk coming off as disingenuous and destroying the purpose of your intention. If you feel yourself preparing to interrupt someone or interject with your own story, think WAIT (Why am I talking?).

Ask yourself:

- Am I talking to demonstrate mastery and to be overly helpful?
- Am I talking to control the situation?
- Am I talking for attention?
- Am I talking to complain?

Here are more productive reasons to talk:

- To ask a follow-up question to understand the person better
- To offer a kind and understanding word
- To share a relatable, empathetic story

Remember that listening and offering a compassionate response is more effective than trying to respond constructively to everything someone says. Gautama Buddha said, "Sometimes it's better to be kind than to be right. We do not need an intelligent mind that speaks, but a patient heart that listens."[4] After someone speaks, take a breath and then respond. It takes time to pause and consider what you want to say and why you're saying it.

With these three steps, you can master setting the groundwork for more intentional Big Talk conversations.

Intentional Living

I once spoke with a man who, facing terminal cancer, shared his personal journal entries with me. He called it the "death zone," where every moment became more intense and intentional. He reflected on how he wanted to be remembered by his kids and how he wished to end his life with "stability, honor, trust, and memories." In his view, dying was a privilege—it was a constant reminder of how to truly live.

What if, one day, a doctor told you that your time was limited? Would you continue with casual encounters and small talk, or would you become more intentional about your time? Would you reach out to the mentor you've been meaning to call, take that trip with your partner, or organize a gathering for loved ones? Life is too short not to be intentional about how we spend our time connecting with others.

Summary

Being intentional requires clearly understanding your purpose in connecting and initiating a conversation. To make a bid for connection, you can share stories, experiences, and accomplishments with others. Set aside time for Big Talk and listen more than you talk.

CHALLENGE: PRACTICE WAIT

Think about someone whom you would like to get to know better. Reach out this week and set an intention to make Big Talk with them and discover something specific and new about them (e.g., their childhood, family, future dreams, or passions). Learn as much about the other person as possible by asking questions related to that specific topic. When it is your time to speak, practice WAIT (Why am I talking?). Ask yourself:

- What is the intention behind what I am about to say next?
- What question could I ask to understand the other person better?
- How can I listen compassionately and let go of my need to talk about myself?

SELF-REFLECTION PROMPT

Think of an upcoming interaction or experience you are anxious or unsure about. Set one to three intentions for that encounter. For example, this could be a conversation with your boss, a session with your therapist, or a phone call with a faraway family member. By setting intentions, you will feel more prepared for the encounter.

INTENTIONAL BIG TALK QUESTIONS TO ASK OTHERS

1. What do you wish we could talk more about that we haven't yet discussed?
2. What do you need help with right now?
3. What have been the highlights of your week?
4. How do you like to maintain meaningful connections with others?
5. What current goals are you passionate about working

on? If you could accomplish anything in the next few years, what would it be?

6. What are some essential life lessons you have recently learned?
7. What values do you live by, and how do they shape your daily life?

INTENTIONAL SELF-REFLECTION QUESTIONS

1. What helps you get into the mindset to have a Big Talk conversation? (For example, it helps me to swim, go on a walk, or journal first).
2. What intentional conversations do you still need to have? Are you putting time into relationships and conversations that matter to you?
3. When are you a good listener? When are you not a good listener?
4. Do you surround yourself with people and experiences that inspire you to stay present? If not, how can you free yourself to explore new and meaningful relationships and encounters?
5. Do you use every interaction to ask new people how they think and feel, or are you too focused on yourself? How can you be more mindful?

5

Share Vulnerable Stories

Someone I loved once gave me a box full of darkness.
It took me years to understand that this, too, was a gift.

—MARY OLIVER, *THIRST*

I love the Japanese art of Kintsugi, a way to mend broken pieces of pottery back together with shining gold paint. The gold seals the cracks, making the piece whole again and highlighting the beauty of the once-broken lines.

As a metaphor for life, Kintsugi shows how we can turn our imperfections (our "cracks") into expressions of ourselves infused with strength, elegance, and history. The next time you feel ashamed of your imperfections, think about how they make you a unique and wondrous human being.

In fact, scars make for great Big Talk conversation starters and stories. Through Big Talk, I've encountered strangers who bravely shared their stories of struggle, like a young man who contemplated ending his life after a breakup, a blind army veteran uncertain about his next steps in life, and a man released from prison, now determined to help youth choose a different path. When I shared these stories with audiences of sometimes millions of people—the response was remarkable. People are moved by vulnerability. They see imperfect, scarred human beings as stunning, sage, and inspiring.

Remember, almost every great story is about transformation through a difficult life experience. The main character starts with an enemy they must conquer—the fantasy trope of a dragon to slay. This dragon is a metaphor for an inner struggle, such as insecurity, grief, or fear. Once the character defeats their enemy, we witness their transformation and the unveiling of their true self.

This familiar, captivating arc is why I skip small talk and ask people, "What was the most difficult part of your life, and how did you get through it?" Their answers reveal the dragon they slayed to become who they are today, showing that by conquering their vulnerabilities, they've become the hero of their own story.

This is me. This is Hazel.

One evening, I strolled on the beach path by the Santa Monica Pier. I saw a tiny older woman sitting on her walker by the sand, observing the ocean. She then took out her phone, turned on jazz music and amplified the volume, stood up using her cane, and began to dance, sliding across the sandy sidewalk in her little black slippers. She was moving and grooving, unembarrassed to dance alone on the sidewalk.

When she stopped dancing, I approached her and complimented her moves. I asked her what inspired her to dance here by herself. She introduced herself as Hazel and said she was eighty-eight years old. She said that ever since her adult son passed away, she dances at sunset almost every day to remember him, celebrate life, and remind herself to have fun and make other people laugh.

> ***Hazel:*** *People don't realize how blessed they are that they are still here!*
>
> ***Big Talk:*** *What was the most difficult time of your life, and how did you get through it?*
>
> ***Hazel:*** *Well, the difficult thing was having my young son. Well, he wasn't all that young, but he was still my baby. He started getting sort of sick. He was going to go into surgery. I says, "Jeffrey, I will go downstairs and get something to eat, and I'll be back up." I got back an hour and a half later, and my son had died. And it was tough for me to understand. Because he had been such a sweet person, he had never been in trouble. He was always trying to help other people.*
>
> *So, I wanted to share this with you: Be kind. If you're not really out there, really touching people's lives, it doesn't make any difference. I get out here and dance every day at sunset, and God knows I make a lot of people happy, laugh, and whatever. So, I just do it. This is me. This is Hazel.*

Through her sunset dance routine, Hazel invites passersby to share a vulnerable moment with her, embrace the collective experiences of grief, and celebrate life. Now whenever I see Hazel, I stop to chat with her and the volleyball players who practice near her sandy dance floor.

If we want others to feel comfortable sharing their vulnerable moments with us, we must take the first step—just like Hazel. We can share a heartfelt story, express our real emotions, or even dare to be a little silly and different. You don't have to dance in public to showcase vulnerability. Vulnerability can shine through when you create emotionally unfiltered art, speak your truth in public forums, ask for help from new sources, or open your heart in conversations with family, friends, and strangers.

You can open up about topic-specific vulnerabilities in a safe and supported space. For example, all over the world, virtually and in person, there are designated support groups that can act as "safe spaces" where people can share vulnerable stories. Some examples include:

- Mental Health Support Groups
- Grief and Loss Support Groups
- Addiction Support Groups
- Trauma and Abuse Support Groups
- LGBTQ+ Support Groups

- Veterans Support Groups
- Disability Support Groups

Many people I've met through Big Talk have found community, support, accountability, and self-empowerment through such groups!

Everyone Is Fighting a Battle

In a podcast interview, someone asked me if I even have a dark side because of my seemingly sunny disposition. I smiled and said, "Of course, everyone has one."

Through Big Talk, I've learned some of the sunniest people I've met have faced the darkest moments in life. People who radiate joy often do so because they've endured profound loss or hardship and now appreciate the sweetness of life. These include parents who have lost children, children who have lost parents, and individuals who once considered ending their own lives. Their smiles don't negate their pain—they're a testament to their resilience.

I once had the opportunity to interview a popular librarian, Mychal, for Big Talk. He had the brightest, goofiest smile and spoke about "library joy." I was taken aback when he shared that he had experienced over 1,800 panic attacks over the course of a few years. Rather than seeing him as weaker, I instantly felt closer to him. I've struggled with panic attacks too, and it's hard to talk about. I was grateful that someone who seemed so joyful, confident, and self-assured was willing to open up about his vulnerability.

Author Regina Brett said, "If we all threw our problems in a pile and saw everyone else's, we'd grab ours back."[1] Believe it or not, everyone is fighting a battle—some just wear it more openly, while others might disguise it behind bright smiles or quiet demeanor. The key is to ask and to listen. Simply asking someone, "What is your current battle?" can open a door to connection and reveal that you're not alone.

Open Up Vulnerable Conversations

If you want to have more vulnerable conversations, it helps to know how to lead the way. When facing a conversation that you know will involve vulnerability, here are some steps to facilitate such a conversation:

1. **Create a comfortable environment for everyone involved.** People won't feel comfortable opening up unless they are comfortable with the setting (place, people involved, and situation). Check in beforehand and ask questions like "Is [X] an okay place to meet? I am also open to your suggestions!"

2. **Model vulnerability.** Be the first to share something personal or heartfelt about yourself. Be open and honest from the beginning. Be genuine and share real thoughts and feelings. People can sense when you're dishonest or putting on a show, while authenticity is powerful and magnetic.

3. **Ask open-ended, feelings-based questions.** Ask questions such as "What's been on your mind lately?," "What

was that like for you?," "How did that make you feel?," or "How did you get through that?"

4. **Listen with empathy and understanding.** Be supportive and nonjudgmental as you listen. Validate their feelings and share any similarities you have experienced. If you connect with them emotionally, let them know nonverbally by maintaining eye contact, nodding, and leaning into the conversation. You can also let them know verbally by sharing your feelings, reflecting on their thoughts, and expressing care.

5. **Acknowledge difficulties and celebrate vulnerabilities.** Show appreciation that the person shared something vulnerable with you and praise them for it. Say things like "It sounds like that was a challenging moment for you—how did you navigate it?" or "That sounds tough. I'm so sorry you had to go through that. I see why you felt that way. Thank you for sharing with me."

6. **Avoid judgment or advice-giving.** Respond with empathy instead.

7. **Follow breadcrumbs.** People may give small clues when they want to share more about something. Be curious and attentive, noticing and following up on things they hint at: "You mentioned that was a life-changing experience—what about it transformed you?"

8. **Be patient and respect boundaries.** Not everyone is ready to share right away. There may be moments of silence

and processing. Opening up is sometimes a long process that can take days, weeks, or years.

9. **Express gratitude.** If someone shares something personal, thank them. Say, "I appreciate you trusting me."

How to Respond When Someone Opens Up to You

If someone shares something personal and delicate with you, it can be hard to know how to respond. You want to be supportive, but you don't want to overstep. You want to say the right thing—but worry about saying the wrong thing.

Here are a few phrases you can use to show empathy:

- "It means a lot that you shared that with me. I'm honored you felt comfortable enough to open up."
- "That sounds really difficult to go through. I'm here for you."
- "That must have taken a lot of strength to endure—and to now talk about. Thank you for trusting me with your story."
- "Please know that you're not alone. How can I support you? Is there someone we can reach out to together?"
- "It's okay to get emotional. You're human, and this is a safe space."

Sometimes, just sitting with someone and listening—without trying to fix or analyze—is the best thing you can do. A simple "I'm with you" might be all that's needed. Silence isn't awkward when it's full of attentiveness and care.

If You Need to Step Back

Some conversations can go deeper than you're ready for. Or you may sense that someone is leaning on you in a way you're not equipped to handle. That's okay. It's important to honor your own boundaries. You can still be kind and compassionate while stepping back.

Here are a few things you might say:

- "I really appreciate you opening up to me. I care about you and want to be honest—I don't think I'm fully equipped to help in the way you deserve. Have you talked to a counselor or therapist about this? I can help you find one."

- "This is a lot, and I can feel how heavy it is. I want to support you, but I might not be in the right space to do that well right now. Can we pause and check in again soon?"

You're not abandoning them—you're being honest. Honesty builds trust.

What Not to Say

When someone gets vulnerable with you, your first instinct might be to comfort them by solving the problem or lightening the mood. But sometimes, those well-meaning reactions can backfire. Here are a few things to avoid:

- **"When that happened to me, I got through it easily. Let me tell you about it."** While relating is important, immediately turning the conversation toward your own experience can feel like you're hijacking the moment.
- **"Stop worrying! You'll be okay!"** This might seem encouraging, but it can pressure someone to rush through their emotions and hold it together instead of feeling what they need to feel.
- **"You don't need to cry."** Tears aren't a problem to fix—they're a natural release. If someone feels safe enough to cry in front of you, that's something to honor.

When in doubt, just hold space. You don't need perfect words—just presence, patience, and permission for someone to be real.

Provide a Sanctuary

In New Hampshire, I met a man named Mark who wore a shirt decorated with colorful hearts and the words "We rise by lifting others." He had come to the park to engage with a man displaying hate flags. Intrigued, I asked about his motivations. Mark shared a story from his time as a mental health counselor, when he was called to be with a couple whose infant had just died. In that moment, unsure of what to do, he simply sat with them, listened, hugged them, and stayed present. Years later, the wife sent a letter thanking him for his compassion, noting that he had followed the procedures in a book on death and dying. Mark reflected, "I was just following my heart." His story was a moving reminder of the impact of quiet, compassionate presence during life's most vulnerable moments.

Mark's experience reminded me that making Big Talk isn't about solving someone's problems or prying into their life. It's about providing a sanctuary where they can share what's in their heart.

Genuine connection comes from maintaining a softness in your heart, even in a complex world. Writer Nikita Gill captures this beautifully: "I will not give up the flowers in my heart just because the world is a hard place. The world is only a hard place because it needs more flower-hearted people."[2]

So, dare to be vulnerable. Ask thoughtful questions, listen compassionately, and create space for others to open up. Sharing and listening heal you and the person you connect with.

Summary

Vulnerability is nothing to be ashamed of. Inspired by the Japanese art of Kintsugi, we see that our vulnerabilities make us unique, resilient, and beautiful. To have more vulnerable interactions, consider opening up more honestly and authentically around people or joining support groups for topic-specific conversations.

CHALLENGE: LEVELS OF VULNERABILITY

Level 1. Gratitude: Think of someone you appreciate but rarely express gratitude to. They could be a family member, a friend, a mentor, or a service worker. The next time you get a chance, let them know why you appreciate them (whether in a handwritten letter, phone call, text, or in-person conversation).

Level 2. Compliment: Compliment someone genuinely. Think of something to say that goes deeper than complimenting their appearance. Mention something about their personality or the way they make you feel.

Level 3. Apology: This is the most challenging thing for so many of us to do. Think of someone to whom you owe an apology. Remember that apologies aren't about changing the past. They are about improving the future. Take a deep breath and share your apology.

BIG TALK QUESTIONS TO ASK TO UNLOCK VULNERABLE CONVERSATIONS

1. What is something you don't often share with others but means a lot to you?
2. What has been the darkest time of your life, and how did you get through it?
3. What is a dream or goal you don't often share?

4. How do you navigate feelings of loneliness or sadness?
5. When was the last time you cried?
6. What is something you struggle with? (Follow-up question) Can I help in any way?

VULNERABLE SELF-REFLECTION QUESTIONS

1. What part of myself do I not usually show to others, and why?
2. What are my weaknesses, and how do I navigate them?
3. What has been making me sad or unsettled lately?
4. When do I feel like the most unabashed, authentic version of myself?
5. What do I love the most about myself? What part of myself do I struggle to accept?
6. What is something I avoid because I'm afraid of failing?
7. What keeps me up at night?
8. What makes me cry tears of laughter, sadness, and awe?

6

Listen with Empathy

Humans aren't as good as we should be in our capacity to empathize with feelings and thoughts of others, be they humans or other animals on Earth. So maybe part of our formal education should be training in empathy. Imagine how different the world would be if, in fact, that were "reading, writing, arithmetic, empathy."

—NEIL DEGRASSE TYSON

At the end of Big Talk workshops, I often ask participants to create and share their own Big Talk questions. During one session, an eight-year-old girl named Penelope raised her hand and asked, "What's something you've missed out on that you wish you didn't have to miss out on?" My heart cracked a little and I felt an empathetic connection to her at that moment. Penelope's question captured a collective childhood experience—our longing to belong. I remembered that everyone wants to feel seen and valued.

With empathy, it becomes harder to cast yourself as the hero and someone else as the villain because you begin to see their struggles, hopes, and joys as your own—making it easier to help one another heal and grow. The first step toward empathy is simple: Talk with each other instead of just about each other.

The universe owes you.

I once approached an older man standing at a local guide booth in the park. He had white hair, piercing blue eyes that matched his bright blue windbreaker, and a friendly grin. He said hello, and I complimented his positive energy. He appreciated the compliment, so I asked him:

> ***Big Talk:*** *What was the nicest thing someone has ever said to you?*
>
> ***He responded:*** *Hmm. Well, I had a fifteen-year-old son pass away in 1994. Three days after it had happened, we were having an early celebration of his life. And one of his friends' grandfathers walked up to me with this accent and said, "You know, I've got to tell you, the universe owes you big time." It always stuck in my mind, what a beautiful thing to say to somebody. It was a very kind moment. There's a hole forever. You learn to live with it.*
>
> ***Big Talk:*** *What were some of your favorite moments with your son?*
>
> ***He said:*** *We were standing up at the rim of the Grand Canyon. His name was Sean. He goes up to the railing and starts to put his foot through the railing. My wife goes, "Sean, come back, you'll fall, stop it." And he turns around and says, "It's okay, Dad will*

fly down and catch me." I'll never forget that. When you lose a fifteen-year-old child—and it's a small fraternity, not that many of us lose teenage children—every moment that you spend with that child becomes a MOMENT. Every moment.

I shared a short video of this conversation on social media, and it revealed the profound power of empathy. Strangers bonded in the comment section—many who had also lost teenage children—offering solace and support to one another in their grief. Others remarked how they could "see the pain in his eyes" and that this video was a great reminder that "all the little moments are indeed the big moments." Witnessing these connections has been profoundly moving and has renewed my faith in humanity.

We are born with an innate level of empathy. The phrase "monkey see, monkey do" comes from mirror neurons, which were discovered by neuroscientist Giacomo Rizzolatti and his colleagues at the University of Parma in the early 1990s, when they saw macaque monkeys imitating one another's behaviors.[1] Mirror neurons are cells in our brains that fire off when we see someone else performing an action or experiencing an emotion. Your mirror neurons might have fired if any of the following have happened to you:

- You saw someone hurt themselves, and you winced as a reaction to their pain.

- Your friend told a joke, and you both started laughing until the laughing escalated, bringing you to tears.
- A baby smiles at you, and you smile back.
- You are conversing with someone, and they lean forward or cross their arms, and you do the same.
- You are at the funeral of someone you do not know very well. When other people in attendance cry, you also feel overwhelmed with sadness.

These mirror neurons help us empathize with others' emotions. You can start practicing empathy by mirroring and listening. Being an empathetic listener requires a certain level of innate compassion and mindfulness, but there are ways we can practice. For example, in his book *The 7 Habits of Highly Effective People*, Stephen Covey outlines four stages of empathetic listening that are related to mirroring:

1. **Mimicking Content:** The listener repeats back the words to the speaker.
2. **Rephrasing Content:** The listener paraphrases the speaker's words, demonstrating that they were actively listening and processing the conversation.
3. **Reflecting Feelings:** The listener focuses on the speaker's emotions and reflects what they perceive to be the speaker's feelings. This stage is a more empathetic approach, requiring you to listen for words and feelings.
4. **Rephrasing Content and Reflecting Feelings:** The listener paraphrases the speaker's statement while reflecting

on their feelings, showing both cognitive and emotional understanding, creating the deepest sense of connection and empathy.[2]

For example, if someone shares with you, "I'm feeling overwhelmed right now. There's too much to do." Here's how you would respond in each stage:

1. Mimicking Content	"You're feeling overwhelmed, and there's too much to do."
2. Rephrasing Content	"It sounds like you have a lot going on, and it's becoming too much to handle."
3. Reflecting Feelings	"You seem really stressed out by everything piling up around you."
4. Rephrasing Content and Reflecting Feelings	"It sounds like life has been overwhelming for you, and you're feeling stressed trying to keep up with everything."

Practicing each stage helps you develop the skills needed for stage four, where you can naturally reflect back both the facts and the emotional experience to a person.

For example, I have a friend who often calls me on a weekly basis in distress. She usually says something along the lines of "I feel like I'm falling behind in every part of my life—grad school, dating, and self-care. I'm freaked out and don't know how to move forward."

I used to respond with something like "Yeah, life is crazy right now. I'm sure next week will be better for you if you just get through this week!" It was a well-meaning response but really just served as filler until she called again the week after. Later, I tried fixing the problem and said, "Have you tried talking to your therapist or working out more in the mornings? Or setting boundaries for yourself?" This solution-oriented response is a common trap where we think we're being empathetic and helpful, but really we're bypassing their emotional experience, and just trying to apply solutions right away.

Eventually, I realized that the best thing I could do was listen with empathy. Now when she calls, I say things like "That sounds so tough. It makes sense you're exhausted, because you're going through so much all at once. I'm here for you. What's been weighing on your mind the most lately?" I learned that being someone who really listens is often more powerful than being someone who fixes. Holding space for someone often helps them feel grounded enough to move forward on their own. Her calls are now less frequent, and our connection is even deeper. When we do hang out, we can open up honestly with each other—and she listens to my problems too.

This shift in our relationship is supported by what psychologists have long observed. Carl Rogers, a pioneer of humanistic therapy, once wrote:

> When you are in psychological distress and someone really hears you without passing judgment on you, without trying to take responsibility for you, without trying to mold you, it feels damn good! . . . When I have been listened to and when I have been heard, I am able to reperceive my world in a new way and to go on. It is astonishing how elements that seem insoluble become soluble when someone listens, how confusions that seem irremediable turn into relatively clear flowing streams when one is heard.[3]

His research emphasized that empathetic listening—being fully present without judgment or interruption—creates the conditions for emotional healing and growth.

Science backs this up too. A study titled "The Neural Bases of Feeling Understood and Not Understood" found that feeling understood activates areas of the brain associated with reward and social connection, which can boost self-esteem and strengthen our sense of belonging.[4] In other words, feeling heard literally helps us feel safer and more confident—sometimes enough to solve our own problems. We don't always need answers. Often, we just need to feel safe enough to be ourselves.

Empathy isn't just something we feel; it's something we practice. It's not always intuitive, and it doesn't come naturally to everyone, especially in a world that often rewards quick fixes over quiet presence. But the good news is that empathy can be strengthened like a muscle.

Here are some small, everyday ways to develop more empathy—both for others and for ourselves:

1. **Immerse yourself in stories unlike your own.** Stories evoke emotion. Read books, watch documentaries, and attend talks or events that explore different lives. Show curiosity by asking questions to deepen your understanding.

2. **Engage with new worlds.** Visit unfamiliar places and organizations. Walk around, observe, and strike up conversations with the people there.

3. **Donate your time and energy to others.** Samantha Power once said, "All advocacy is, at its core, an exercise in empathy."[5]

4. **Observe your judgment in real time.** Catch yourself the next time you notice yourself silently judging someone—a stranger, someone you read about, a friend, a coworker, or even yourself. Pause and ask: What struggle, pain, or fear could be beneath the surface? This shift in inner dialogue grows self-awareness and compassion. Even better, ask them about what they're going through.

5. **Ask better questions.** Instead of a canned "How are you?," try:

   - "What's been on your mind lately?"
   - "Is there something you want to talk about that you haven't had a chance to share?"

6. **Use empathetic language in everyday conversations.** When someone shares something difficult, try phrases like:

   - "That sounds really difficult."
   - "You're not alone in this."
   - "What can I do to support you?"

Bonus: The Empathy Challenge

One of my best friends has political views that are different from mine. We've managed to stay close by listening to each other, asking thoughtful questions, and maintaining mutual respect. During one of our conversations, she challenged me to name three things I liked about a political candidate I strongly disliked.

At first, I saw red. *How could I say anything good about this awful person?* But I took a breath and really thought about it. To my surprise, I was able to name three genuine things I appreciated. That simple shift cracked open space for understanding—and it stayed with me. Now, whenever I feel strong negative emotions toward someone, I return to this exercise. It helps me move from judgment to curiosity.

Try it:

1. Think of someone you disagree with or feel tension toward.
2. Name three things you genuinely appreciate about them—big or small.
3. Consider how they might feel about you, before and after doing the same challenge.
4. Observe any shift in your feelings toward them.

Remember, you don't have to agree with them. Just notice the parts that remind you we're all human—and that there's always more to the story. You might find yourself even growing fond of someone you originally disagreed with. As Mary Pipher wrote, "Empathy can turn contempt into love."[6]

If you continue to practice empathy in your interactions and conversations, you'll become the friend someone calls in their darkest moments, the coworker they trust to express their concerns to, or the neighbor they turn to for support in times of need. Empathy in our daily relationships lays the foundation for creating positive change on a societal level. It's the force that inspires someone to travel halfway across the world to aid in disaster relief or to donate to a fundraiser for a stranger battling cancer. By stepping into unfamiliar environments and connecting with others, you'll develop empathy and have more

Big Talk conversations. You'll skip the surface-level small talk to dive into conversations that foster understanding, compassion, and deep emotional connections.

Summary

Empathy is the ability to connect to others by understanding and sharing their feelings. Empathy comes from being open-minded, an attentive listener, and being able to reflect someone's experiences to them.

CHALLENGE: BUILD EMPATHY

1. **Explore a stranger's story.** Spend an afternoon in a quirky café, train station, or park. Observe a stranger and craft a story about their life—imagine their struggles, triumphs, and relationships. If you feel comfortable, strike up a conversation and see how much of your imagined story aligns with their lived experiences.
2. **Understand an opposite perspective.** Think of someone with a viewpoint that challenges your own. Instead of debating or dismissing them, seek resources like books, articles, or interviews exploring their perspectives. Journal about what you've learned and reflect on how this process impacts your feelings toward them. Then, if you can, talk to them and ask to hear their story and perspective.

3. **Help out a community.** Volunteer for a day at an organization that supports a community different from yours. Whether it's serving meals, tutoring, or assisting at a shelter, immerse yourself in their world to understand and connect.
4. **Listen quietly.** Spend a day with someone from a different background or life stage, but challenge yourself to listen far more than you speak. Ask thoughtful questions and hold back from giving advice or comparing their experiences to your own.

BIG TALK QUESTIONS TO ASK TO BUILD EMPATHETIC CONNECTIONS

1. What have you been thinking about or feeling a lot of lately but haven't had a chance yet to share?
2. When do you feel the most safe and understood?
3. What has been on your heart recently?
4. When did you last feel genuine joy? When did you last feel genuine sadness?
5. What is a life lesson you learned through a difficult time?

EMPATHY SELF-REFLECTION QUESTIONS

1. What is something difficult you overcame that you're proud of?
2. What has been on your own heart recently?

7

Speak with Sincerity

You never know when a moment and a few sincere words can have an impact on a life.

—ZIG ZIGLAR, *RAISING POSITIVE KIDS IN A NEGATIVE WORLD*

A few years ago, I had a disagreement with a friend who lived on the other side of the country. Instead of addressing it, we both avoided talking to each other for months. Then, one day, I called her. First silence. Then—"This has been really hard for me," she said. "Me too," I replied. "I didn't know what to say because my feelings were complicated." At that moment, we realized how avoiding the truth and genuine communication led to unnecessary tension and wasted time. But when we finally expressed our feelings, we found a way to resolve the conflict.

Being sincere can help clear misunderstandings and forge strong bonds. Sincerity is the sister of vulnerability. While vulnerability requires revealing something delicate about ourselves, sincerity involves a level of candor that sometimes might be uncomfortable. Both require expressing genuine thoughts and occasionally tricky emotions, but when embraced, they can foster intimacy and create lasting connections.

Some examples of sincerity include offering a genuine apology, such as "I'm sorry I hurt you," or expressing heartfelt appreciation, like "Thank you for being there for me." It could also mean giving credit where it's due, as in "If it weren't for you, it would have been hard to complete the project," or answering a question honestly—for example, "I would love to, but I have been a little burned-out and feeling down lately." These acts of honesty and authenticity deepen trust and strengthen relationships, creating a foundation for meaningful connections.

It's been the hardest thing in my life.

In September of 2024, I visited New York for two weeks. While walking, I met a woman who said I reminded her of her granddaughter. We started to move past small talk, and I asked her about her family. How many children and grandchildren did she have? How often did she see them? She said one of her children is estranged. I didn't ask her why. I just asked her:

> ***Big Talk:*** *How are you getting through that difficult time?*
>
> ***She said:*** *Well, it will make me cry. We have only one daughter, and she is a lovely young girl. About seven years ago, she brought back some complicated stuff,*

and now she will not see us. That is still ongoing. It is such a deep sadness. It has been a hard lesson. Accepting and respecting her feelings has been the hardest thing in my life.

This woman openly and gently revealed something that many people experience—estrangement—but don't dare talk about. These moments of sincerity and vulnerability feel louder and more significant than others in my life. Why? Because they are so full of presence, authenticity, and meaning.

While sincerity may feel abstract as a concept, here are some practical ways to cultivate it:

Use Humor to Express Sincerity

Comedians are a particularly sincere group of people. They are like the person at a party who blurts out what everyone is thinking but no one has the guts to say out loud. Even when it's off-putting, they have an authenticity that can draw us in.

Maybe we delight in comedians because they so openly confess to being fully, unapologetically human. There's a certain duality in the humor and sadness they articulate, often revealing truths about themselves and the world. Comedian George Lopez captured this well when he said, "In life, there's a yin and a yang and a balance. And when you don't have balance, you have comedy."[1]

So many of us walk through life trying to appear even and balanced. The truth is, few of us are, but we rarely admit it. Humor can be a bridge to authenticity, making it easier to share what's going on beneath the surface.

For example, if someone asks, "How have you been lately?" you might respond with: "Well, lately I've been waking up with a racing heart and wondering who signed me up for skydiving in my sleep!" In that moment, humor becomes a vehicle for sincerity in admitting struggles with anxiety, allowing you to express vulnerability in a way that feels approachable and human.

Actions Speak Louder Than Words

Sincerity is more than what we say and how we say it; it's also what we do to show we care. Actions reflect our true intentions. To me, there's nothing more genuine than someone who follows through on their promises or offers a gesture of kindness without expecting anything in return.

One day, I met a man outside my apartment who had walked from Honduras to California, searching for gardening work. As we spoke, he shared that his sister had passed away from cancer and that he was now living on the street. Moved by his story, I told him to wait one moment. I ran inside to grab some food and money for him. When I returned, I saw him buying a tie-dyed women's Grateful Dead T-shirt from another man experiencing homelessness. With a warm smile, he handed the shirt to me and said in broken English, "Don't worry, it's clean!" His generosity, giving me something when he had so little, reminded me that sincerity doesn't always come in grand gestures—it often shines through in small, heartfelt acts.

Think about the glowing moments of kindness and sincerity you've experienced—someone remembering to call you back, listening to you vent during a tough time, offering help without you asking for it, remembering a detail like your favorite dessert, or simply being present when you needed them. These moments resonate because they are sincere. There's nothing more beautiful than when someone shows up with their whole heart.

Treasure Each Encounter: *Ichi-go ichi-e*

Miracles are around you every day, but sometimes you might be too busy to notice them. The Japanese idiom *ichi-go ichi-e (一期一会)* translates to "one time, one meeting" or "one encounter, one opportunity."[2] It reminds us to treasure every moment because each is unique, fleeting, and unrepeatable. It challenges us to show up fully present and appreciate the significance of every single opportunity in every interaction.

How do you make something ephemeral last forever? We never get the same moment twice. So, how do we make it count? The key is to make each moment memorable and meaningful. For example, you might wake up one morning after a gray winter spell and find yourself marveling at a soft, pale blue sky. Instead of going through your usual routine, take ten minutes to step outside. Notice how the roses have finally bloomed, how sweet they smell, and how radiant they look framed against the sky. Take a snapshot in your mind and soak in the moment of appreciation.

In the context of Big Talk and sincerity, *ichi-go ichi-e* reminds us that every conversation holds deep and endless potential. We may never meet the same person under the same circumstances again, not even those we see every day. People change, moods shift, and so do we. That's why even brief moments can leave a lasting impact—like a friend's unexpected kindness or a stranger's words that echo in your memory for years. When I lived in Singapore for ten months, I kept a journal titled *Moment*, where I recorded every meaningful moment and encounter I remembered—because I wanted to treasure them forever.

It's vital to bring our whole selves to every interaction. Understanding that the moment might never repeat means we should be honest, heartfelt, and authentic in how we relate to one another to make the moment more meaningful. I love the poem "Don't Hesitate" by Mary Oliver, where she reminds us that joy isn't something to ration. When it arrives—suddenly or unexpectedly—we should welcome it fully, without hesitation. Even in a world that can feel unkind or overwhelmed by sorrow, greed, or uncertainty, there's redemption in allowing joy to take up space. Whether it's a moment of love, a quiet glimpse of beauty, or a meaningful connection, we should let it move us.[3]

A Sincere Life

Sincerity is about demonstrating genuine presence and care through a heartfelt conversation, a shared activity, or a simple gesture of compassion. It's about avoiding autopilot—treating people and moments as routine or insignificant—and instead practicing intentionality.

When we understand the fleeting nature of time and connections, we can approach life more openly and authentically. Sincerity, paired with attention and thoughtfulness, turns fleeting encounters into profound experiences. Practice *ichi-go ichi-e*. Show up sincerely, speak honestly, and act with intention. By doing so, you'll create deeper connections and ensure that the moments that matter don't slip by unnoticed.

Summary

Being sincere means expressing yourself authentically and intentionally. *Ichi-go ichi-e* is a beautiful reminder to be present and sincere in each experience, encounter, and conversation because each moment is once in a lifetime.

HOW TO PRACTICE SINCERITY

1. **Practice presence.** Practice being fully present in your next conversation or interaction by eliminating distractions such as your phone, multitasking activities, or wandering thoughts. Express your emotions and answer questions honestly.
2. **Ask genuine questions and listen actively.** Before asking someone a question, ask yourself, "What do I genuinely want to know about them?" rather than "What do I think I'm supposed to ask them?" Then, ask accordingly. Listen to them without preplanning your subsequent response. Notice their words, their tone of voice, and their body language. These are all parts of what they are trying to tell you.

3. **Express emotions authentically.** If you feel something, don't hold back. Express your genuine emotions in that moment to create a more heartfelt exchange.

4. **Be kind without an ulterior motive.** Help or compliment someone without expecting anything in return. You will feel lighter and at peace.

5. **Reflect.** What did you learn from your day, your conversations, and yourself? By being in touch with your feelings and thoughts, you will reflect more sincerely on the world.

CHALLENGE: SINCERE CONVERSATION STARTERS

The next time someone asks you, "How are you?" or "How have you been?" try to refrain from giving an automatic answer of "Good and you?" Consider how you have been, and offer a sincere conversation starter. For example:

- Highlight something happening in your world by being vulnerable and reflective: "I'm okay—I have been navigating the loss of my pet. Have you ever gone through a period of grief, and have any tips?"
- Mention something specific: "I feel inspired to paint again after my recent trip. I might start with painting a mural on my wall. What's been exciting in your world?"

SINCERE BIG TALK QUESTIONS TO ASK

1. What crucial lesson have you learned in the last few years?
2. What is a momentous decision you made that led you to where you are today?
3. When do you feel most authentically like yourself?
4. What are you grateful for in your life right now?
5. Who do you want to get to know and why?
6. What value do you hold onto that you wouldn't compromise for anything?

8

Self-Reflect Often

Knowing yourself is the beginning of all wisdom.

—ARISTOTLE

On Monday mornings, I go for a walk alone in the woods. It's how I reset and ground myself before the week begins so I can be fully present for others. There's one eucalyptus tree grove I love—its fresh scent, the crunch of leaves below my feet, and shimmering spiderwebs clinging to branches in slanted light. If I'm feeling uninhibited, I hug a tree. This place is my sanctuary, where a ten-minute walk easily becomes thirty.

As I walk, thoughts move like waves stirring up sand, shifting and clearing. I reflect, make plans, and jot notes on my phone. These walks slow me down, opening space for chance encounters.

My Monday walks have become a ritual, a rare moment of solitude free from obligations. In Asia, I discovered *shinrin-yoku*, or forest bathing, which is a practice of going out into nature not for exercise but for presence. Not everyone has access to a forest, but finding your ritual for self-connection is essential. Your sanctuary might be a bike path, a pottery studio, a temple, a hilltop, or even a quiet corner at home—anywhere you can find clarity to slow down.

Science supports this. A ninety-minute walk in nature lowers activity in the prefrontal cortex, the part of the brain tied to rumination, freeing the mind for peaceful and creative reflection.[1] In other words, giving yourself a mental reset allows you to check in with yourself and be more attuned with everything you have going on. Self-reflection is a catalyst for change. Many of my most powerful Big Talk conversations happen with those who have undergone a transformation—people who have slowed down with introspection and reshaped their lives with intention.

Do the work.

At a friend's dinner party one evening, I met a young man named Joaquin. He seemed like one of the happiest people I had ever met, with sandy hair, eyes that twinkled like aquamarines, and a playful grin. He was interested in my work, so I asked him to make Big Talk. We met the next day at one of my favorite parks, a small grassy hill overlooking the ocean:

> *Big Talk: When was the last time you cried tears of joy?*
>
> *Joaquin: Wow [starts tearing up]. What's difficult about that is I've gone through a really dark period in my life in the past few months. And I've only cried*

tears of sadness, not tears of joy. So I wish I could tell you when the last time was. And that's kind of what just made me upset. It was probably as close as four weeks ago; I contemplated not being here anymore. I was going through a lot of stuff; I lost someone very close to me, and it could have been very easy to give up. And I'm proud that I took the initiative to get therapy, to "do the work," and start having a more positive outlook. But I think what I'm most proud of right now is the fact that I didn't give up and that I'm still here.

Big Talk: *I'm glad you're here too. You know what's interesting—I didn't ask you, "When was the last time you cried tears of sadness?" because you seem like such a joyful person.*

Joaquin: *It just shows that you never know what people are dealing with on the inside, no matter what they put out on the outside. So I think it's super important to be kind and respectful to people.*

Joaquin's Big Talk was illuminating. I had no idea that he had gone through so much pain. I am grateful he did the self-reflective work to come out on the brighter side of life.

Self-reflection strengthens your connection with yourself and others. When you are able to pause and look inward, you gain deeper insight into your emotions, motivations, and values. This awareness empowers you to be authentic and fosters a greater sense of presence, allowing you to connect more meaningfully with those around you.

Self-Reflection Practices

The following is a list of exercises and practices that will help you tune in more to yourself, for it is through being self-aware that we are in the best position for Big Talk.

1. Take a moment each day for gratitude and reflection.

When I go on Big Talk sunset walks, I take a moment to check in as the sun is setting. I ask myself (and whomever I'm with at that time):

- "What little things brought you joy today?"
- "What are three things you are grateful for in this moment?"
- "What are you looking forward to?"

This exercise helps me maintain self-awareness, presence, and an optimistic mindset. It's also a way to make Big Talk with my sunset companions, leading to meaningful conversations and memories.

Try to find a time and place each day to express gratitude and reflect on your day, whether at sunset, while commuting home from work, over dinner, or before bedtime.

2. Ask yourself, "What matters most?"

The Stanford Graduate School of Business asks MBA applicants each year to answer, "What matters most to you, and why?" in their first essay.[2] You don't need to apply to business school to benefit from this self-reflection prompt.

In your own journal, answer this question: What matters most to you, and why? You can have more than one answer. Then ask yourself the follow-up questions:

- Am I leading my life according to what matters most to me?
- If I am not, what steps can I take to adjust my life?

If you're having difficulty reflecting on this question, remember to remove the pressure to have it all figured out. Instead of asking questions that seem like mountains to climb, ask questions that are smaller hills. For example, instead of asking, "What do I want to do with my life?" ask, "What do I currently feel most inspired to explore?"

3. Write Morning Pages.

In *The Artist's Way*, author Julia Cameron repeatedly recommends writing "Morning Pages" every morning—three pages of stream-of-consciousness writing without inhibition. I started this practice and can attest that it is an excellent form of self-reflection.

- Page one is about getting your swirling thoughts—the "monkeys in your mind" out of the way.

- Page two is for organizing your thoughts. Sometimes, I write lists and frameworks of thought on page two.
- Page three is for letting yourself reflect deeply as a human being. Be wild and free! Page three is where new ideas and revelations start to take shape.

Start practicing journaling in the morning at the time that works best for you. I find journaling most effective after I've had a cup of coffee and a short, technology-free walk in my neighborhood.

4. Understand the urgent / important matrix.

The Eisenhower Matrix allows you to sort out tasks by what is most urgent and/or essential in your life.[3] It helps you eliminate what is unnecessary and instead focus on the long-term outcomes of your daily tasks. Try filling this out:

	Important	**Not Important**
Urgent	What is important and urgent?	What is urgent but not important?
Not Urgent	What is important but not urgent?	What is not urgent and not important?

Once you can focus on what is important and urgent in your life and prioritize what is important but not urgent over what is urgent but not important, you will feel like a more aligned version of yourself.

5. Know your big rocks.

One example I love about prioritizing what's important is Stephen Covey's "Big Rocks" metaphor.[4] He tells you to imagine a container representing your ability to get things done. You can either fill it with big rocks (the things that are most important to you, such as family, health, personal time, and passion projects), little rocks (minor tasks and responsibilities), or sand (distractions).

The problem is that most of us fill our containers with so many little rocks that we don't have room for our big rocks, leaving us unfulfilled. The key is to start with your big rocks and then fill the extra space with little rocks. Take control of your time and focus on your priorities. You will have more time for experiences and relationships you care about rather than living a life reactive to distracting societal demands.

Try reflecting on what your big rocks are. Notice: What little rocks are taking up your time and space?

6. Make time for creativity.

One of the best ways to self-reflect is to create. Whether you enjoy cooking, DJing, woodworking, writing, painting, playing music, assembling vision boards, filmmaking, gardening, or DIY home improvement, creative expression will help you connect with your innermost self. It helps you explore ideas and emotions and leads to a sense of deep intrinsic fulfillment. It also puts you in flow.

I like watercoloring and practicing piano. My sister embroiders and makes fine jewelry, my mom sews quilts, and my dad loves assembling photo collages of our family gatherings. One of my friends writes slam poetry. I met a man who carves chess pieces out of wood and another who makes surrealist collages out of old magazines.

Find a medium that works for you, and find time each week to have a creative date with yourself.

7. Exercise and stretch.

Regular exercise and stretching help you maintain a healthy body and reduce stress. When your mind-body connection is intact, you are more grounded and can connect with yourself. Start by incorporating stretching into your daily routine. Make sure you breathe and focus on each movement and moment.

8. Journal about what keeps you up at night.

Writing can offer a sense of control in a world that often feels unpredictable. While everything around you may be swirling with uncertainty, putting pen to paper helps anchor your thoughts in the present. It gives you space to name your fears, process your emotions, and let your feelings spill out—honest and undiluted.

Prompt: *What's one thought or feeling I've been carrying lately that I haven't had space to fully explore?*

Where Self-Reflection Meets Big Talk

Self-reflection deepens your relationship with yourself, strengthens connections with others, and sets the stage for Big Talk. When you're self-aware, you show up as your genuine self, and that encourages others to do the same. This kind of authenticity builds trust and connection.

When you're in tune with your own emotional experiences, it's easier to understand and relate to others. One afternoon, I met a woman who was the voiceover actress for Ash Ketchum—from one of my favorite childhood shows, *Pokémon*. She was radiant and funny, so I expected our conversation to be lighthearted—since we were talking about a cartoon. But instead, she opened up about how hard it had been to carry that responsibility in her twenties—a turbulent time when she didn't yet know who she was. The pressure of the role kept her from fully experiencing joy until much later, in her thirties, after a lot of self-reflection and therapy.

Rather than being surprised and trying to steer the conversation back to cartoon characters, I found myself relating to her. I shared how I, too, had struggled during my twenties and only recently began to truly appreciate the impact of my work through Big Talk—and the simple joys of life. Because we had both done the inner work, we were able to skip small talk (though we did talk about our favorite cartoon characters!) and connect on a deeper, more vulnerable level.

Self-reflection leads to personal growth and is also essential in conflict resolution. When I struggle with a friend or family member, I first journal about it, asking myself: "Why do I feel triggered?" and "What can I do to process or cool off so I can approach the conflict with empathy, rather than defensiveness or blame?"

Learning from our experiences and applying those lessons helps us evolve, bringing more depth and meaning to our relationships. And isn't that what it's all about—cultivating relationships that inspire growth, trust, and connection?

Summary

Self-reflection is a necessary step toward connecting with others. First, you must connect with yourself to foster empathy, awareness, and authenticity. This will create space in your life for genuine connections.

CHALLENGE: SELF-REFLECTION ACTIVITIES

Find your self-reflection sanctuary. Then, explore each self-reflection activity mentioned in the chapter (perhaps choose one per week) and slowly build your favorite practices into your daily routine.

1. Take a moment each day for gratitude and reflection.
2. Ask yourself, "What matters most?"
3. Write Morning Pages.
4. Understand the urgent/important matrix.
5. Know your big rocks.
6. Make time for creativity.
7. Exercise and stretch.
8. Journal about what keeps you up at night.

SELF-REFLECTION QUESTIONS TO ASK YOURSELF:

1. What brings you pure peace and joy?
2. If you could accomplish just three things in your life, what would they be?
3. What do you struggle with in life? How can you work on it?
4. What do you love about your life?
5. What are some values you currently live by?
6. What can you do to lead a life that's more authentic to who you are?
7. What matters most to you?
8. What do you worry about the most, and why?
9. What do you hope others will remember about you at the end of your life?
10. What are you most afraid of, and what is that fear stopping you from doing?
11. What character traits do you respect the most in others that you wish to embody yourself?
12. What does the weather in your mind look like? Is it foggy or stormy? What would it take to make it clear as a crystal blue sky?

9

Cultivate an Open Mind

An open mind leaves a chance for someone
to drop a worthwhile thought in it.

—MARK TWAIN

During the Los Angeles fires in 2025, I met with Miss Dorothy, a ninety-seven-year-old woman visiting the remnants of her burned-down home in Altadena. She stood up from her walker, looked at the rubble, smiled at me, and said, "Isn't this funny? I'm looking at this, and I don't see this disaster. I see the good times and all the memories!"

Never before had I met someone with such grace and open spirit. I believe her outlook contributes to her longevity. Like Miss Dorothy, give yourself the freedom to remain open to life—to its opportunities, joys, triumphs, failures, devastations, celebrations, and changes.

A person who seeks joy and beauty will find it everywhere—they'll delight in the sound of rain tapping on the window and the cozy feeling of staying indoors during a storm. But someone focused on negativity may wake up and think, "How dreary, another rainy day." Similarly, someone who views strangers as potential friends will greet others with warmth in their smile and eyes, making it easier to connect with them. In contrast, a person who sees strangers through a more hostile lens will miss out on opportunities to connect.

Make friends with perfect strangers.

I usually fly with TSA PreCheck, but on one flight, I forgot to add my TSA number to my boarding pass. I was stuck waiting a little longer than usual in the security line. That's when I noticed an older man standing behind me, his baseball cap signaling that we probably had very different political views. I nervously smiled and used the time waiting in line to work on my phone. But then the man leaned over my shoulder and said, "Damn, how do you type so fast?" I laughed and replied, "I'm used to it. Do you ever have to type on your phone for work?" He said, "I do. My daughter helped me start making TikToks. I give life advice and stuff." I couldn't resist. "Life advice! I love hearing people's perspectives on life. Could I interview you?" He introduced himself as Bear, and though my flight was boarding by the time I'd made it through security, we decided to do the interview anyway.

Big Talk: What are you proud of in life?

Bear: My marriage of thirty-two years and counting.

Big Talk: What's the secret?

***Bear:** Forgiveness. Understanding that I'm a human and she's human. We all make mistakes, and we have to forgive each other. That's my proudest thing.*

***Big Talk:** What do you want to do before you die?*

***Bear:** What do I want to do before I die? Oh my gosh. I don't know. I've done it all. I've been to Alaska. I've been all over Canada. I've been to Hawaii. I've been to Europe. I've been to Mexico. And I've met so many good people. I think the one thing that I want to do before I die is meet more good people.*

***Big Talk:** What advice would you give to the younger generation?*

***Bear:** Understand that without love, you have nothing. Love each other. We all have to live together. We all have to be friends with each other. Make friends with perfect strangers.*

***Big Talk:** What's been a challenging part of your life, and how did you get through it?*

***Bear:** My dad, just a few days before he died—He said, "Son, I think I'm going to die." I said, "No Daddy, you're not going to die. You're going to live forever." He said, "Well, I wish you'd tell me how that's going to happen." I said, "Daddy, you're going to live forever because you're going to live through your sons and* *the sons that your sons have and the sons that they shall have." And I think that gave him some peace.*

Online, I would have never naturally connected with this man who might have had different political views than I did. But because we met in person and started talking based on family, kindness, and relationships, we formed a genuine bond. I encourage people to look beyond religious and political differences and remain open-minded enough to connect on our shared human experiences—just as Bear and I did.

From a scientific perspective, it may seem easier to be closed-minded in the short term. Sticking to what's familiar reduces fear and uncertainty. It allows our brains to ease cognitive load.

However, we can cultivate open-mindedness through neuroplasticity—the brain's ability to adapt. Neuroplasticity means that our brain constantly rewires itself in response to new experiences and learning, regardless of our age (there's a common misconception that we stop adapting after age twenty-five). Even as adults, we can form new neural connections, break old patterns, and change how we think and respond to the world. So yes, even an old dog *can* learn new tricks!

Your upbringing may also play a significant role in your level of comfort with novelty. You may naturally be more open-minded if you were raised in an environment that encouraged curiosity and exploration. On the other hand, if you grew up in a more insular environment, it may take extra effort to develop open-mindedness.

Here are some ways to practice becoming more open-minded:

1. **Try something new.** Attend an event outside your usual interests and be open to learning. Visit a new place, explore a different culture, or sign up for a class. Stepping into unfamiliar situations will push you outside your comfort zone and help you become more adaptable. When I was a kid, my dad would pick a different cultural event from *LA Weekly* each week. We ended up at a Filipino festival, a strawberry festival, a Beatles celebration, and even a radio show taping. This helped me become comfortable entering unfamiliar spaces where I was the "outsider."

2. **See the world like you're on vacation.** Approach people with the same curiosity, respect, and open-mindedness you would show if you were traveling in an unfamiliar place. When I travel, I love engaging with locals, asking about their lives, and learning about their experiences. It's an easy way to practice curiosity and expand your perspective.

3. **Ask questions and listen without judgment.** When you come across unfamiliar ideas, ask questions to understand them better and express your curiosity without judgment. It's okay to disagree, but showing interest in others' experiences and beliefs helps you grow. For example, you might ask, "What life experiences have shaped your beliefs?"

4. **Build friendships with diverse people.** Surround yourself with friends from different backgrounds, beliefs, and experiences. This will broaden your worldview and deepen your capacity for empathy. I love spending time with friends of all ages, from an eleven-year-old I

"babysit" (who's also a great Big Talk partner) to my eighty-eight-year-old martial arts friend (a black belt!). Each relationship teaches me something new.

5. **Engage with nonfiction media.** Listen to podcasts, read books, watch documentaries, and engage with media that challenge your perspective or spark your curiosity. Every week, I try to watch a documentary about a topic I know little about, which keeps me open to new ideas and viewpoints.
6. **Explore fiction.** Fiction is a powerful tool for expanding open-mindedness. Through stories, we safely explore new worlds, ideas, and people, growing in empathy and understanding. Fiction lets us walk in others' shoes without judgment.

While having a closed mind might feel more relaxing, in the long run, an open mind encourages flexibility and enriches our lives. To have an open mind, it is essential that we refrain from being judgmental and seeing ourselves as superior to others or as always "right."

Avoid "Holden Caulfield Syndrome"

It's easy to relate to book characters because they often verbalize our hidden thoughts. Reading is perhaps the closest thing to telepathy that we have.

During my late teenage years, I read J. D. Salinger's 1951 novel, *The Catcher in the Rye.* I, along with many other young adults who read this book, empathized with the main character, Holden Caulfield. Throughout the book, Caulfield observes that everyone around him seems "phony," so he alienates himself from people, choosing to be a loner. Although some of his behavior in the book is extreme, Holden is relatable as an angsty young adult jaded by a superficial world.

I've nicknamed Caulfield's pattern of self-isolation, judgment, and interpersonal avoidance "Holden Caulfield Syndrome." It's easy for a modern-day adult to feel jaded by the information overload of political messaging, unnecessarily provocative media content, and incessant marketing. The temptation to declare the world irreparably sour and fake and withdraw into bitterness can be strong.

To avoid this trap and recognize and reaffirm that there is good in the world and in people, it's essential to recognize the symptoms and take proactive steps to combat them.

Symptoms and Treatments for Holden Caulfield Syndrome

SYMPTOM: CYNICISM

If you look at people through a lens that filters them into two categories, "phony" or "genuine," it will be too easy to fixate on the negative. Your standards for authenticity are thus going to be impossibly high. Our brains have a negativity bias in which we respond more intensely to negative stimuli and often spend more time thinking about negative events and emotions.[1] If cynicism becomes a habitual response, we will fall out of practice in facing the discomforts of uncertainty and vulnerability and lock ourselves into a cycle of negative thinking. This mindset can make people withdraw and turn inward, rejecting the world rather than engaging with it. We see this in the trope of the grumpy neighbor who never wants to step outside to say hello because they hate people, or the disgruntled teenager who thinks the whole world is against them.

TREATMENT: REFRAME YOUR THOUGHTS AND SEEK GENUINE CONNECTIONS

The key is to reframe your thoughts and instead ask yourself, "What do I see in this person that is good? How can I engage with that part of them and learn more about where they come from?" Seek to form real and meaningful connections with others and invest in genuine relationships. Instead of being cynical from afar, talk to people up close and in person. Be open to seeing others' shortcomings, fears, and hopes, and let them see yours. Although it can feel safer to isolate, connection is what will make you more empathetic, connected, and happy.

SYMPTOM: EMOTIONAL ISOLATION

Holden runs away and isolates himself from school, his parents, and himself. In running away, he builds a wall around himself and is unwilling to connect with others. While emotional isolation can seem like a form of protection, it actually involves constructing a prison around yourself. This prison is made of loneliness.

TREATMENT: SHOW VULNERABILITY

To break down those walls, we must be willing to share our emotions with others and face the fear of disappointment and vulnerability, knowing that the benefits of feeling seen and understood are worth it. Acknowledge that sometimes the world isn't fair and doesn't make sense. But rather than retreating into bitterness, lean into the feelings of vulnerability and reach out to others. Find meaning in the messiness of life through the support of people who are also going through it.

SYMPTOM: POINTING FINGERS

The title *Catcher in the Rye* comes from Holden's fantasy about saving children from falling into the corrupt adult world. Yet, in his journey to save others, Holden neglects to address his issues and save himself. It's easy to point fingers at the world and everything wrong with it rather than confront our own problems and broken parts. We see people lashing out in social media comment sections and review sites all the time, only to click on their profiles and realize they are far from perfect themselves. In pointing fingers, we shift the blame and avoid self-growth.

TREATMENT: BALANCE IDEALISM WITH REALISM

It's easy to point out all the flaws in the world and see others as less than ideal. But the key is first to accept that people are not perfect, that they might disappoint you, and that you might even disappoint yourself. Then, choose to engage with others anyway and live your life to the best of your ability while acknowledging that sometimes we all make mistakes. Every time you find yourself internally or externally criticizing someone else, instead ask yourself, "What good am I doing by pointing fingers?" and "What are some things I can work on to be a better person in this world?"

SYMPTOM: FEAR OF CHANGE

Change in all shapes can be scary: growing up, moving to a new city, making difficult choices, leaving people we are familiar with, and facing the uncertainties of the world at large. Like Holden, many of us cling to the idealized versions of our childhood selves when we were blissfully ignorant and didn't have to make so many decisions. But clinging to your past will stunt your ability to move forward in life.

The fear of change is often rooted in the fear of failure or facing our shortcomings.

TREATMENT: EMBRACE DISCOVERY

We can all relate to the fear of change. Yet resisting it won't make life any easier. Change is our only constant. So instead of fearing uncertainties, we can embrace the discovery of something new and celebrate the evolutions in our lives. Ask yourself, "What risks do I want to take that I have been putting off? What are the consequences if I fail, and how can I gracefully recover from them?" and "What transitions am I uncertain about? What am I looking forward to about them?" Be open to change, and new opportunities and connections will bring joy to your life!

Accept Our Complex World

It's easy to see the world in simplistic terms: genuine or phony, good or bad, clean or messy. People are introverted or extroverted, tall or short, wise or stupid, nice or mean. It's easy to be a critic. But real life is nuanced. The key is learning to live in the gray area, accept the many contradictions of the world, and strive to understand one another with empathy. Only then can we begin to have real conversations with one another.

I've spoken with individuals on the fringes of society. While they may have made choices that led them down a difficult path, they are also human beings who've shared with me their unconditional love for their children, their awe at seeing the ocean for the first time, and their dreams of reconnecting with loved ones. It takes courage to live authentically in an imperfect world. The goal isn't to avoid feeling disillusioned—it's to avoid letting disillusionment define you. If we strive to be open-minded, we can more easily embrace complexity and change and make lasting connections with others.

Summary

Nurturing an open mind allows us to view the world with less hostility, connect more easily with others, expand our perspective, and adapt more readily to change.

CHALLENGE: SEE THE WORLD THROUGH A CHILD'S EYES

Children are the most open-minded among us. They approach the world with curiosity, free from many of the restrictions and biases we learn as we grow. They'll talk to and play with anyone, regardless of background, and they aren't afraid to ask questions about things they don't understand. To embrace a childlike perspective:

1. **Leave room for wonder.** Ask questions about the world around you. Simple activities like walking in nature, visiting a museum or new neighborhood, or stargazing can inspire awe and wonder!
2. **Explore new ideas.** If something doesn't make sense to you, instead of closing yourself off to it, be exploratory and playful. Ask fun questions that help you maintain an open mind and explore, like "There

must be really good reasons why someone is into this. Let's find out!" Join an activity, talk, meeting, or event that will help you to better understand the subject.

3. **Be curious about everything.** Ask why, how, and when about anything that sparks your curiosity.

4. **Be playful.** Adopt a playful spirit. Playfulness allows you to think of normally stressful things in a more manageable and optimistic way. For example, sometimes when I'm trying to solve a problem, I draw and paint possible solutions with watercolors.

OPEN-MINDED BIG TALK QUESTIONS TO ASK

1. What's something you learned recently that surprised or delighted you?
2. What belief or value do you hold that may differ from how others think?
3. What is something people might misunderstand or not know about you?
4. How has your worldview evolved over the years?
5. What is a part of your culture or childhood that you wish more people understood about you?
6. What do you enjoy or experience in your life that you wish more people would try with you?

10

Focus on What Matters Most in Life

Remembering that I'll be dead soon is the most important tool I've ever encountered to help me make the big choices in life. Because almost everything, all external expectations, all pride, all fear of embarrassment or failure—these things just fall away in the face of death, leaving only what is truly important.

—STEVE JOBS

Whenever there is terrible turbulence on an airplane flight, I have the sudden urge to check in on the person next to me and grab their hand—regardless of whether they're my travel companion or a total stranger. My first human instinct when faced with the possibility of "going down" is to connect with another human being. I'm sure I'm not alone in this.

Most people do not want to die alone, but as we age, the hours we spend alone often increase. That's why it's vital to nurture the foundation of connection through communication and building meaningful relationships. Establishing these bonds early creates a sense of support and belonging, which can help us navigate loneliness and strengthen our well-being as we grow older.

Our relationships are what tether us to earth. In 1938, during the Great Depression, Harvard University launched what would become one of the longest-running studies on human development in history. Researchers set out to discover what makes us truly happy. Over more than eighty years, the results have consistently shown that happiness and health don't come from wealth, fame, or hard work—but from meaningful relationships. In fact, the study found that how satisfied people were with their relationships at age fifty was a better predictor of their physical health later in life than even their cholesterol levels. People with strong social support or loving partners were better able to face physical challenges with emotional resilience—because they knew someone had their back. Psychiatrist George Vaillant, who led the study for several decades, summarized it simply: "When the study began, nobody cared about empathy or attachment. But the key to healthy aging is relationships, relationships, relationships."[1]

That's why when I attend traditional networking events, instead of asking myself, "Who should I meet that can help me become more successful?" I ask, "Who here has a kind and warm demeanor that I'd love to become real and lasting friends with?"

We make each other laugh.

One morning, I spotted two older women wearing turtlenecks, sitting on a bench, and sharing a laugh across the street from my home. I recognized them because they often stroll together in the mornings. I said hello and asked if they were sisters. They laughed and said they were longtime friends. Their names are Barbara and Anne.

Big Talk: *How long have you known each other?*

Barbara: *Seventy-five years.*

Anne: *We went to grammar school and high school together. So we're both eighty-seven years old. We both lost our husbands, and that brought us even closer together. Now, Barbara lives right next door to me. So we're hooked into each other every day, which is a good thing because in old age, it's nice to have friends around you. If you have people and friends around you, it may give you a younger frame of mind.*

Big Talk: *What's the key to sustaining a friendship?*

Anne: *You know, the true test of a friendship or any relationship is: Can you travel together? She's very funny, and I'm a good audience member.*

Barbara: *We laugh at the same things. For example, that car going by doesn't have a driver in it. I mean, we can never get over that. We just laugh so much. We get a kick out of each other. We get a kick out of the people we meet, and we have met quite a few with our walks.*

Millions saw the video I recorded of this conversation with Barbara and Anne. Many people commented that friendship is the most fundamental thing we need in life and that they wished they would one day live next door to their best friends.

When I first started Big Talk and walked up to strangers to ask them, "What would you do if you knew you were going to die tomorrow?," one of the answers that stood out to me the most was from a young woman on the beach: "I would go on a road trip to see someone, and finally tell them that I love them." I wondered why she hadn't told them yet. Maybe she was waiting for the "perfect moment."

Reflecting on our mortality can motivate us to focus on what truly matters, pursue what we've always dreamed of doing, and build the relationships that mean the most to us. On average, we have about 29,000 days to live—365 days a year, with 24 hours each day.[2] If we spend eight hours sleeping and another eight hours working, we're left with just eight hours a day to live on our terms.

One exercise for reflecting on what really matters to you is reading obituaries. By exploring the summaries of lives well-lived, you can gain insight into the values and experiences that resonate most deeply. This reflection can help you clarify how you want to live your own life and recognize what might be holding you back.

However, before we can fully embrace what matters most, we must first understand the barriers that keep us from doing so. Below are a few common obstacles, along with Big Talk questions to help navigate them:

Why People Avoid What Matters Most to Them

Fear of failure: Some people are so afraid of failure that they do not even begin following their dreams. However, if they don't start, they may forever live in a space of yearning or regret. We can build a vision of failure that isn't even in line with reality. Mark Twain once said, "I've had a lot of worries in my life, most of which never happened."[3] This reminds me of the hours I spent ruminating on "What ifs" and "Should I be doing this?" questions instead of just taking action. Next time you find yourself in such a mental loop, ask yourself:

> *What would I do if I could not fail? What would it mean to fail? If I do fail, what will I have learned?* (Hint: If you learned something, it's not failure.)

Waiting for the "perfect moment": I can think of a few people who don't have the liberty of biding their time or waiting until the perfect moment, such as people with terminal illnesses or those with demanding jobs. If your hours are limited, then so is your ability to dillydally. However, it is essential to remember that we are not promised tomorrow, and there is no better time to begin than now.

> *What would the perfect moment look like? If I stopped waiting for "perfect," what could I start doing now to pursue my goal?*

Lack of resources: It can be challenging to pursue what we care about without time, support, or money. Sometimes, that stops us from trying.

What resources do I need to achieve my dreams? What steps can I take to start achieving them?

Distraction and procrastination: External distractions, such as other people's requests, entertainment, and the news, can prevent us from focusing on what matters. We must set boundaries and learn to say "no" (respectfully) to others and ourselves.

How much time am I spending on distracting activities? What can I replace those activities with that aligns more with my goals?

Is anyone taking up my time with whom I need to set a boundary? How can I do so politely but firmly?

Disorder: Sometimes, we need to remove messiness and excess from our lives to make time for what matters to us. If you're surrounded by disarray, stressed out, or in go-go mode, it's hard to focus on your relationships and loftier goals. Once we realize what matters most, we can focus on nurturing our relationships, prioritizing our health, and living according to our purpose.

What can I clear from my life? (Emails, meetings, dishes in the sink, and closets are all examples.)

Is there anything I need to reorder and prioritize?

So If Relationships Are What Matter Most—How Do We Deepen Them?

It starts with how we communicate with others on a daily basis. Small talk can help us break the ice, but it's Big Talk that builds the bridge to long-lasting, meaningful relationships. Big Talk is about asking deeper questions that create space for vulnerability, understanding, and true connection. You don't need a perfect setting or profound words—just the courage to be curious and the willingness to listen. A single, thoughtful question like "Who has shaped you the most?" or "When in your life have you felt most connected to someone?" can turn an ordinary moment into something unforgettable. If we want to focus on what matters most—feeling supported as we age, growing closer to the people we love, and living a meaningful life in line with our values—we need to intentionally practice connecting on a deeper level with the people around us.

Time Is All We Have—and Don't.

We are responsible for our time, relationships, and how we lead our lives. Sometimes, it takes a sobering moment to finally focus on what matters: surviving an accident, losing a friend, being fired, or the death of a loved one. When we grieve, small talk seems superficial. Having been close to death, loss, and real heartbreak makes one refocus priorities. Take these moments to reflect and share/give love rather than withdraw from the world.

Remember that two of the things people crave most in life are purpose and love. No matter where we are in the world, we all share the same desires—to find joy, to be happy and healthy, and to feel secure and loved. We seek strong relationships, peace, purpose, and something to work toward and hope for.

I'll end with one last exercise:

Imagine yourself at one hundred years old.

You're looking back at the last one hundred years of your life.

Who holds a meaningful place in your heart?

What are you proud of?

Where did you spend your time?

What do you wish you had done?

Which memories warm your soul?

Which ones leave you cold?

Who do you want to spend more time with?

(Make time for those people and things today.)

Summary

Remembering what matters most helps us achieve our goals, strengthen our relationships, and live life according to our most actualized selves. We can then limit distractions and devote our time to Big Talk conversations and actions that lead us to the people and directions of our dreams.

CHALLENGE: WHO MATTERS MOST?

Think about who matters most to you in your life. Write a list of names and a few sentences about what they mean to you. Then, over the next few hours, days, and weeks, make sure you set up time to see them and spend meaningful, uninterrupted time with them. For some, this might mean having weekly family dinners or calls with mentors. For others, this might mean scheduling a yearly trip with their best friend who lives far away.

BIG TALK QUESTIONS TO DISCOVER WHAT MATTERS IN YOUR LIFE:

1. What would you do if you knew you only had five years to live?
2. Who and what in your life makes you feel the most alive? Why?
3. What's a dream or goal you've put off? What's stopping you from pursuing it?
4. What would you regret not doing if your life were over tomorrow?
5. What do you want to be remembered for?
6. If you could spend a day doing anything without limitations, what would it be?

7. What's a moment when you felt truly connected to something bigger than yourself?
8. What values guide your decisions, and how do you embody them daily?
9. What's a cause you would dedicate your life to if resources and time weren't a barrier?
10. Who do you most want to express gratitude to, and why?
11. What's something you've always wanted to make, build, or create, and what's holding you back?
12. What makes you lose track of time in a good way?
13. What, to you, is a life worth living? Reflecting on the last week, what moments come to mind in which you felt you were living your best life? What are the moments when you felt you were wasting your time?
14. What lesson have you learned from loss or failure that changed how you moved forward?
15. How do you define a full and meaningful life?
16. What are you most proud of in your life, and why?

11

Practice Kindness

Something deep in the human soul seems to depend on the presence of kindness; something instinctive in us expects it, and once we sense it we are able to trust and open ourselves.

—JOHN O'DONOHUE, *TO BLESS THE SPACE BETWEEN US*

One morning, as I was walking back from the post office, I saw a teenage girl being verbally harassed by a man on a bicycle in broad daylight. She stood there frozen, unsure of how to respond. I felt a surge of protectiveness and decided to step in. I walked up to the man, calmly and firmly told him to "leave her alone," and, gently putting my arm around her shoulder, guided her to a more public space. She broke into tears, thanking me for stepping in. I stayed with her at a nearby bagel shop while she called her dad, and we waited together until he arrived to pick her up.

Later that evening, an elderly woman approached me, speaking Spanish, and asked when the bus would come. I told her there were no more buses, and her face filled with concern. I offered to give her a ride home, and she trusted me, gratefully getting into my car. She thanked me several times before I dropped her off at her gate.

That day brought me quiet joy and an unexpected sense of fulfillment. It reminded me of the power of random acts of kindness and human connection and how even the smallest gestures can have a meaningful impact on others and ourselves.

I was reminded of Ben Franklin's morning ritual—waking up and asking himself, "What good shall I do this day?" and thinking I should apply it more often. Now, I try to start my days by focusing on the good I have the potential to put out there.

Start planting apple seeds.

While visiting a park with a friend and sitting on the limbs of an old tree, I asked her, "What do you think life is about?" Suddenly, a small, blond, blue-eyed boy climbing the tree above us peered down. His face was smeared in dirt that caked his rosy cheeks. His name was Atticus. He climbed down from the tree and, like an old soul, he shared with us:

> ***Atticus:*** *I think life is about Love. Helpfulness. What else? Thankfulness. Hope. Joy. Earth. Anything good for other humans.*
>
> ***Big Talk:*** *Do you know what you want to be when you grow up?*
>
> ***Atticus:*** *Yes. I want to be a person who makes the world a better place and gives people homes.*
>
> ***Big Talk:*** *How old are you?*

Atticus: *I am six.*

Big Talk: *Do you want kids one day?*

Atticus: *Yes, I really want kids.*

Big Talk: *When you have kids one day, how will you raise them?*

Atticus: *I would raise them as good kids that help around and help people. Maybe when they grow up, they could teach their kids about what I taught them, and then when those kids grow up, they could teach their kids what they learned about, and that's what I want to do.*

Big Talk: *Is there anything else you want to say?*

Atticus: *Maybe one more thing. I would say that trees and everything in life can make the world a better place. Like if you had a bunch of tomato seeds, or maybe apple seeds, you can put them in the ground, and start planting them.*

This six-year-old boy possessed the wisdom that so many people seek. He reminded us of the importance of paying it forward—"planting our seeds"—and watching them grow to help others one day. If everyone were as kind and thoughtful as little Atticus, I'm sure the world would be a more compassionate place.

Kindness touches all aspects of life—from realizing the value of nurturing a tiny seed in the ground (like Atticus) to understanding our role as human beings in relation to others and the vast universe.

If you're like me and have ever been awestruck by the concept of outer space—wondering how we can exist in an ever-expanding universe—you've probably heard of Carl Sagan. An American astronomer and renowned science communicator, Sagan was celebrated for his reflections on humanity's relationship with the cosmos.

In his famous speech "Pale Blue Dot," inspired by an image of Earth taken from space, Sagan reminds us that we earthlings are but a tiny, granular dot in an immense universe. Referencing the picture of Earth, he says:

> That's here. That's home. That's us. On it, everyone you love, everyone you know, everyone you have ever heard of, every human being who ever was lived out their lives. . . . Every king and peasant, every young couple in love, every mother and father, hopeful child, inventor and explorer, every teacher of morals, every corrupt politician, every superstar, every supreme leader, every saint and sinner in the history of our species lived there—on a mote of dust suspended in a sunbeam.[1]

Carl Sagan's ultimate point in "Pale Blue Dot" is that astronomy is profoundly humbling. Recognizing that we are responsible for caring for our tiny planet reminds us to tread gently. As Sagan famously said, it is our responsibility "to deal more kindly with one another, and to preserve and cherish the pale blue dot, the only home we've ever known."

Sometimes, a simple statement of love, appreciation, or wonder is all it takes to brighten someone's day—or inspire them to pass that kindness on. So, try complimenting people more often. It's easy to comment on surface-level things like appearance—"You're really pretty" or "I like your shirt." But to turn small talk into Big Talk, compliment something deeper. Compliment their essence, their soul.

I still remember a compliment someone gave me on a bus ride over ten years ago. They said, "You seem to have eyes that shine and reflect more light on the world than anyone I've ever met. What makes you so happy?"

Here are some examples of thoughtful compliments paired with Big Talk follow-up questions:

- **"You have an uplifting smile.** What brings you so much joy in life?"
- **"I love your sense of humor; it's so refreshing!** How did you develop such a great outlook?"
- **"You have kind eyes.** What has influenced your kindness?"
- **"You're a great listener, and your advice means a lot to me.** Is there anything on your mind that you'd like to share with me?"
- **"The world would be a better place with more people like you.** What do you think we can all do to make the world a little kinder?"
- **"You're like a sunbeam—every room lights up when you walk in!** Have you always had this brightness about you, or was there a moment that brought it out in you?"

- **"Your presence is so calming—thank you for that.** Where do you go, or what do you do to find your own sense of peace?"
- **"I appreciate your deep empathy.** Would you be willing to share more about how you navigated [X experience]?"

These thoughtful compliments, paired with curiosity, will make people feel genuinely appreciated! The next time you want to compliment someone, try thinking of a way to make it more thoughtful with a follow-up question.

Surround Your Life with Kindness

If you struggle to see the beauty and good in others, it might be time to reflect on your surroundings. Are you surrounding yourself with kind and compassionate people? Seek out the ones dedicating their time to compassionate causes—feeding those experiencing homelessness, fighting fires, healing and caring for others, collecting donations for people in need or animal rescues, participating in support groups, gathering in welcoming spaces, teaching their skills to others, or tending to a community garden.

We can only notice wonder or grace in the world if we've made space for it in our own minds and hearts first. Hold good images in your thoughts, and you'll start to see more good around you. When negativity creeps in, try redirecting that energy toward kindness instead. Borrow it from time spent fixating on bleak news headlines or anxious thoughts. Borrow it from the hours you spend alone on a

Saturday afternoon watching television and redirect it toward showing up at a community park cleanup or first aid training.

Small, intentional shifts in your perspective can help you cultivate a more positive outlook and inspire kindness in yourself and others.

Here are some examples:

- If you read an article criticizing someone and feel the urge to join in with negative comments, pause and ask yourself, "How would they feel? What positive or kind thing could I think about them or the situation instead?"
- If someone cuts you off while driving, and you feel road rage bubbling up, try something different. Give them a nod and a smile instead. You'll feel the weight of negativity lift as you let it go and move on with your day.
- If you are impatient and waiting in a long line, start a friendly conversation with someone waiting with you instead of complaining. Make a joke and say, "Where would you rather be right now?"

Develop Kindness Rituals and Gestures

I encourage you to develop your own personal brand of simple acts of goodwill. For example, when my husband and I go to the beach, he always picks up trash from the ocean and tucks it into his bag or wet suit to dispose of it later. In high school, I had a friend who baked a cake for everyone's birthday without fail. I keep water bottles, snacks, and dollar bills in my car so that whenever I see someone in need on the street, I can offer them something.

It turns out that it's better for your well-being to give gifts to others than yourself. Research by psychologist Elizabeth Dunn found that spending money on others can lead to greater happiness than spending it on oneself. This phenomenon, known as the "warm glow" effect, suggests that giving gifts or helping others can boost your own well-being.[2]

Going out of your way to show gestures of care can lead to Big Talk. A woman I met in a Facebook group for female surfers commissioned me to paint a portrayal of her late mother swimming in the sea. Rather than mailing it to her, I decided to travel to Carlsbad to hand-deliver the painting. When she saw the image of her mother gliding through the ocean, she burst into tears of gratitude. This moment was meaningful for both of us. We shared a conversation about her mother and our mutual love for the ocean. I'll never forget the sincere appreciation on her face. I'm so grateful I made the trip to meet her in person.

One way to combine kindness with Big Talk is to offer small gifts as acts of generosity and conversation starters. For instance, I once gave my postman some oranges I had harvested from my family's garden, and I brought over my foster puppy to my gardener, offering him a joyful and playful break! Now, I can break the ice and have friendly conversations with the people I see every day.

Brainstorm your own acts of kindness, whether they involve mentoring people at work, baking for neighbors, or reading to kids at a hospital. The key is finding a way to contribute to the world that feels authentic to what you care about. You'll find that being kind is fun! These acts—big or small—help you feel more hopeful, optimistic, and connected while making the world a little brighter for others. Such gestures can transform someone's day—and even their perspective. Sometimes, they can turn a whole community around!

Five Easy Ways to Practice Kindness

If you've been feeling down about the world lately, one of the quickest ways to lift your spirits is to lift someone else's. Here are five simple ways to help others, uplift yourself, and create bonds of connection:

1. Create a kindness kit.

The next time you go to the grocery store, break a ten or twenty-dollar bill into singles and buy some water bottles and a box of healthy snacks like granola bars. Keep a stash of these snacks and dollar bills in your car or bag. That way, you're ready to offer something tangible when you see someone experiencing homelessness and asking for help. When I do this, I look the person in the eye, greet them as a friend, and ask them, "Would some water, a snack, and a couple dollars help?" I can tell you—there are few feelings more moving than when someone looks at you with eyes sparkling with gratitude. In that moment, you can feel the power of connection.

2. Commit to a volunteer shift.

Sign up to volunteer somewhere one week from now. Whether it's an animal shelter, park cleanup, or community garden, committing ahead of time will make you more likely to follow through. Search for local nonprofits or community service opportunities to find inspiration and resources.

3. Check in on a struggling friend.

Think of someone you know who's been going through a hard time—maybe they're grieving, burned-out, or just unusually quiet. Send them a message or give them a call. Ask how they're really doing, offer to talk, and remind them you're here for them. Sometimes just knowing someone cares makes all the difference.

4. Offer practical support.

If someone in your life is struggling—physically, emotionally, or mentally—offer specific help. For example:

- Take them to a doctor's appointment.
- Treat them to dinner after a breakup.
- Join them for a walk in nature and just *listen*.
- Help them look up professional resources.

Small actions can be a huge relief to someone going through a tough time.

5. Write a note of appreciation.

Think of someone who's positively impacted your life—a teacher, mentor, friend, or even a barista who always remembers your order. Write them a thank-you note or a heartfelt message. Expressing gratitude not only boosts their day—it boosts yours too.

Spreading kindness goes hand in hand with building human connection. After all, kindness is an exchange of energy—and it often happens through interaction with others. Those small moments of care can soften hearts and open the door to deeper conversations, even Big Talk.

Summary

It is easier to practice kindness when you realize you are just a tiny part of an infinite universe. Offer compliments and compassionate gestures, and surround yourself with kind people. Being kind improves your mental health, strengthens your relationships, and builds empathy. Kindness creates a ripple effect, hence the phrase: "Kindness, pass it on."

CHALLENGE: 30 DAYS OF KINDNESS

Day 1: Smile at every stranger you pass by today. Avoid the urge to look away or at your phone.

Day 2: Compliment someone today and ask them a follow-up question.

Day 3: Purchase a coffee or treat for someone else, either a friend, mentee, or someone behind you in line. (You can tell them you are trying a kindness challenge—they will be pleasantly surprised!)

Day 4: Call an old friend to catch up and hear how they are doing.

Day 5: Write a thank-you note to someone who has helped you.

Day 6: Donate items you no longer need to friends, people you meet, or a charity.

Day 7: Write a positive review for a small business, service, or restaurant you love.

Day 8: Offer to go out of your way to give someone a ride, walk with them to where they need to go, or simply wait with them at a bus or train stop.

Day 9: Comment something kind on a stranger's blog or social media post.

Day 10: Help a neighbor with errands or tasks such as gardening, grocery shopping, or chores.

Day 11: Cook for someone or bake yummy goods and give them out to neighbors, friends, charities, or people experiencing homelessness.

Day 12: Help a coworker or classmate with something, even if it's not your burden.

Day 13: Compliment someone about their character or personality (not just their appearance).

Day 14: Donate even a tiny amount to a cause you are passionate about.

Day 15: Leave a positive note in a café, library, or community space for the next person who finds it.

Day 16: Check in on someone you know who might feel lonely or down.

Day 17: Pick up trash on the beach, in a park, or in your neighborhood.

Day 18: Make a piece of art for someone.

Day 19: Write a handwritten letter to a distant family member or friend.

Day 20: Help tend to a garden or plant something.

Day 21: Buy flowers for someone you love—or even a stranger!

Day 22: Compliment someone's hard work.

Day 23: Visit an animal shelter and sign up to walk the dogs or foster an animal.

Day 24: Help an individual who is living on the street.

Day 25: Reach out to a mentor or teacher to express gratitude.

Day 26: Give a snack or treat to a delivery person or post office worker.

Day 27: Share something you love (like a book or hobby) with someone who might enjoy it.

Day 28: Talk to someone who looks lonely.

Day 29: Offer to help someone with their professional goals—whether that's reviewing their résumé or pitch, recommending them for a job, or sharing their work.

Day 30: Start a conversation with someone new—ask a meaningful question—make Big Talk!

KINDNESS-THEMED BIG TALK QUESTIONS TO SELF-REFLECT ON OR ASK SOMEONE

1. Can I help you with something you're struggling with?
2. What is the kindest thing someone has ever said to you?
3. What is the kindest thing someone has ever done for you?
4. What is your favorite compliment you have received?
5. How do you show kindness to yourself?
6. Who is someone who inspires you to be kinder?
7. What is a small act of kindness someone performed that inspired you?
8. What can you do to spread and expand kindness in your own life?

12

Remember, Everyone Has Something to Teach You

A single conversation across the table with a wise person is worth a month's study of books.

—CHINESE PROVERB

When I was in college, I asked one of my mentors the original Big Talk question: "What do you want to do before you die?" I expected a bold answer to match his bold personality, so I was surprised when he simply responded: "To have more good days." His answer has stayed with me. Instead of chasing grand experiences or the next adrenaline rush, I realized the importance of appreciating each day as it unfolds. I will always be grateful to my professor for that realization.

There are lessons to learn from everyone, everywhere. Some of the most profound insights arise during interstitial moments of life—the small, often overlooked pauses between more significant events—waiting for a train, walking between meetings, or the quiet gaps between scheduled errands. Though they may seem insignificant, these moments provide valuable opportunities for reflection and connection. These are the times when I journal, process my thoughts, or engage in Big Talk with others. During these instances, I often find the most connection with others and within myself.

I appreciate learning from people who have more years of life experience. Conversations with older individuals provide wisdom and a much-needed chance for connection, something many older people may lack in their daily lives. For those who are retired or living alone, human interaction can often be limited to brief exchanges. Taking a moment to listen to their stories can make them feel seen, valued, and appreciated. I often ask older people, "If you could share a message with the younger generation, what would it be?"

I have three secrets.

In the fall of 2023, I stopped to chat with a radiant older woman walking along the beach path. She wore red lipstick and a straw hat and went by "Babs." I asked her:

> *Big Talk: How old are you?*
>
> *Babs: I'm ninety years old.*
>
> *Big Talk: Wow! What's your secret?*
>
> *Babs: I have three secrets which I would like to tell you because young people are always in a hurry to live life and don't necessarily take good care of themselves. The first rule I have is to move your body well. The second rule is to feed your body well. And the*

third rule, the most important of them all, is to rest your body well.

Big Talk: *What life lesson would you pass on to the younger generation?*

Babs: *Life lesson? Never quit. Have a bucket list. Make sure your life is interesting. I was sixty years old when I was offered a job in Europe, and number one on my bucket list was to live there. Always have a goal, and if you have a setback, just wait. Because good things come, and bad things come. But the bad things do pass, and you can just open another door.*

Big Talk: *What's still on your bucket list?*

Babs: *Oh, unfortunately, I can't do what's on my bucket list at my age. I wanted to visit Greenland, Iceland, or Alaska to see the aurora borealis—the northern lights.*

The video of our conversation went viral on Instagram with over thirty million views, and soon offers from Iceland Air and hotels around the world poured in, inviting Babs to come see the northern lights. At first, I couldn't quite understand why her advice resonated so powerfully across the globe. But then I began to hear Babs's simple wisdom echoing in my own mind. When I felt myself burning out, I remembered her gentle reminder to "rest your body well." I started taking naps, stretching more, and making time to slow down. I also began to "feed my body well" and "move my body well"—choosing fresh fruits and vegetables over junk food, and committing to martial arts and surfing.

I realized that Babs's wisdom extends beyond the body; it applies to our minds too. We must move, feed, and rest our minds well to take care of our mental health and be prepared to make Big Talk.

Sometimes, simple words of advice have the power to transform you. These words echo more vividly in your soul when you hear them from someone who speaks to you directly and looks you in the eye rather than from an anonymous source.

See the Equal Signs

I once took a self-defense seminar from my Taekwondo teacher. He visualized one way humans tend to compare themselves. He said that we subconsciously look at people with an equal, less-than, or greater-than sign hanging over them.

When we see someone with an equal sign, we tend to gravitate toward them and want to befriend them. When we see them with a greater-than sign, we either look up to or fear them—sometimes avoiding them. When we see someone with a less-than sign, we might feel inclined to ignore them or pick on them.

If you're one of the people who tend to look at people with a less-than or greater-than sign, try practicing looking at them with an equal sign instead. There is no need to idolize a greater-than-sign person or pity a less-than-sign person. We are all human, after all, and we have the same innate drives in life. Treat everyone with respect—and also like a potential friend.

The next time you catch yourself distancing yourself from someone, ask yourself what it would be like to live a day in their shoes. What are their hopes, thoughts, and worries? What can they teach you about life?

Think of Big Talk questions as equalizers that level the playing field, offering everyone a chance to share their thoughts and experiences, no matter who they are or where they come from.

Find the Hearts in Everything

Life lessons, unique stories, and whispers of wisdom are found everywhere. You just have to remain open-minded, inquisitive, and kind.

A few years ago, I walked through the Venice neighborhood of California. A few blocks from the beach, on a busy street, there was an encampment for people experiencing homelessness. I saw a small, older woman in a floral dress sweeping the concrete sidewalk outside her tent, accompanied by a black-and-white spotted dog.

I said hello. Her name was Jerry. I asked her what in life had led her to her circumstances. She shared that her husband left her, and she lost her home. But she said, "What I learned is there are two things we possess in life, and that's your heart and your soul. The rest is just stuff. So we go forward and do the best we can."

She then showed me her collection of "hearts" and pulled out her most recent find—a stone in the shape of a heart. She said she sees hearts in folded paper, stones, and tree shapes and saves them.

Our conversation moved me to tears. Jerry had no more than a tent on the street. She chose to see the hearts instead of the pain in her life. Her mindset, despite her circumstances, showed me that people are capable of so much strength and love.

Jerry taught me to "see hearts"—to always look for love and hope. The next day, I returned to bring her a watercolor set because she said she used to paint.

Stop and Watch the Rockets

Another day, I went for my usual sunset walk. I ran into a man I recognized who lived down the street. He was looking up at the sky. I said hello and asked what he was looking for. He said a rocket launch was coming soon. I asked him how he knew, and he excitedly pulled out his phone and showed me his Rocket Watch app.

A small crowd began to gather as he taught us about rocket launches. I just loved how this man nerded out about a specific subject and taught it to all of us passersby who stopped to listen. We all waited and watched the launch together over the horizon. It was a beautiful reminder to stop and smell the roses (or watch the rockets!) and learn from someone else.

Take a Moment for the Little Things

While visiting a shady park, I noticed a man feeding peanuts to squirrels. He offered me a handful to share with them too. I hesitated, then asked how often he did this—and why.

He told me he started feeding squirrels to take a break from the chaos of the day. It helped him slow down, focus on the little things—literally—and feel more connected to nature.

I told him I was touched by his gesture and shared a bit about Big Talk. We said goodbye and went our separate ways. That evening, I received an email from him. He wrote: "I too wish people would consider the bigger questions in life. Please keep going. It's good to know you're out there."

I felt the same about him. It was comforting to know there are people out there quietly caring for nature and our smaller neighbors. He helped me remember the importance of pausing—of stepping away from the noise—to show compassion and presence for the world around us.

Through Big Talk encounters with strangers, I have learned that everyone has something to teach us if we just take the time to stop, say hello, and learn about who they are.

Summary

Remember that everyone, no matter who they are, where they are from, or what they have been through, has something to teach you about life if you are curious and open-minded.

CHALLENGE: A WEEK OF LEARNING

Day 1: Express curiosity for something someone is doing or learning about. Ask them to teach you what they know. For example, if a friend is into watching documentaries, ask them what they've learned. If someone is studying martial arts, ask them to teach you a new self-defense move.

Day 2: Walk into a bookstore or a library and ask for the current staff member's recommendations. Talk to them about what they learned from reading. You can also ask friends, community members, and family for book recommendations.

Day 3: Sign up for a class, lecture, or workshop from a local expert. You could explore singing, public speaking, marine conservation, foraging, personal finance, foreign language skills—the possibilities are endless!

Day 4: Ask a service worker what they enjoy doing outside of work and how they became involved in that activity.

Day 5: Ask a family member or friend about their life philosophies. Take the time to sit down and discuss with them. Ask them, "What are your favorite values, teachings, or sayings?" If you have an older acquaintance, family member, or mentor, ask what advice they would give the younger generation and what experiences have led them to that perspective.

Day 6: Learn something new that gets your adrenaline up, like rock climbing, surfing, snowboarding, or white water rafting.

Day 7: Join a volunteer opportunity and learn about a new cause and why people are passionate about it.

BIG TALK QUESTIONS TO ASK AND LEARN FROM OTHERS

1. What life lesson have you learned recently?
2. If you could give advice to the younger generation, what would it be? How does that draw from your personal experience?
3. What is a setback that taught you a lesson?
4. What are your current interests and hobbies? Can you teach me about them?
5. What are you currently nerding out on? Do you follow anything? Collect anything?
6. How do you handle self-doubt, fear, or failure?
7. What causes or beliefs are you passionate about?
8. What is a dream you are working toward?

13

Communicate Through Challenges

Most people do not listen with the intent to understand; they listen with the intent to reply.

—STEPHEN R. COVEY, *THE 7 HABITS OF HIGHLY EFFECTIVE PEOPLE*

The 2024 U.S. election was heated and divisive. Hateful and impulsive comments flew like daggers across the ether of the internet from every direction. I heard people say things like "If you voted for [X], never talk to me again!" I reflected on the divide and realized how little I knew about the other half of the country—the people who had voted differently than I had. By chance or maybe a little nudge from the universe, I started to meet people with opposing views everywhere I went. I met them at airports, on art walks, and in my neighborhood. Only by the end of our conversations did their political leanings surface. They didn't seem hateful at all!

I decided to approach our conversations like an anthropologist—with curiosity and humility instead of judgment. By leading with an open mind, I found that many of these individuals were kind and thoughtful—they just saw the world differently because of their unique upbringings, life experiences, and personal motivations. I discovered that when I spoke to these people in person—not through the filter of news clips or social media—we shared many of the same desires. We wanted people to be better listeners. We wanted peace. We wanted to revive the simple, warm-hearted values of helping our neighbors.

I promised myself that I would prioritize listening to real people over listening to what the media wanted me to think about people. By setting aside judgment and approaching others with curiosity and understanding, I could build genuine connections.

Some combination of yin and yang.

Every year, I visit Kentucky to see my dad's side of the family. One of my uncles, Uncle Lee, always arrives late to dinner—just in time for dessert. With his bushy white beard and quiet demeanor, he's a man passionate about rare instruments, Tai Chi, and philosophy. I realized that, like me, he wasn't one for small talk. One year, we sat down together and had a much deeper conversation.

> ***Big Talk:*** *What are you proud of, Uncle Lee?*
>
> ***Uncle Lee:*** *Probably raising my son. When he was about five years old, he was diagnosed with autism spectrum disorder. He grew up being a difficult child to raise—stubborn and resistant to authority. He later appreciated that I made him stick to values like learning how to deal with other people. You know you*

can't always have your own way, and your way may not always be the right way for everybody. And to understand other people's views. I think Tai Chi has taught me to go with the flow more and try not to be too resistant, to be flexible, but also to be aware of protecting yourself while being open to other people. Some combination of yin and yang, which I think is very prevalent throughout the universe.

Through this simple but profound conversation, Uncle Lee reminded us that communication isn't always easy. Stick to your values while also making space to go with the flow and listen to other people.

We all live in separate realities, shaped by our personal histories, identities, and environments. Once you accept this, it becomes easier to embrace others as they are—and to appreciate what makes you uniquely you.

Rather than dwelling on our differences, finding common ground leads to more meaningful connections. After all, no one ever sees themselves as the villain in their own story, which is why arguments often go nowhere. Even criminals sometimes view themselves as heroes, writing manifestos to justify their actions.

So, consider the beliefs you hold dear—ones that others may not share. How likely is it that someone could truly change your mind? And how much more would you respect them if, instead of trying to persuade you, they listened, sought to understand, and responded with empathy?

Below, I've outlined strategies to help you communicate effectively through differences and challenges.

Write a "Lincoln Letter"—A Letter You'll Never Send

In July 1863, President Abraham Lincoln was deeply frustrated with General Meade's hesitation and failure to capture General Lee's army after the Battle of Gettysburg—an opportunity that might have ended the Civil War. Disappointed, Lincoln wrote a strongly worded, emotionally charged letter to Meade.

But Lincoln never sent it. Why? He understood the importance of letting his emotions settle. Instead, he wrote "Never Sent" on the letter and tucked it away in a drawer.[1]

When you're feeling angry or emotionally overwhelmed, one of the most effective things you can do is write a letter and not send it. This simple act helps you process your emotions while avoiding unnecessary conflict or escalation with others. This is an effective strategy to use after a bitter breakup, before a tense conversation with a family member, or when communicating dissatisfaction to a boss or business partner. Once your emotions have settled, you can have a calmer and more productive conversation with someone.

On a similar note, when I started writing this book, I was given this advice: "Write the first draft for yourself, the second for a friend, and the third for a critic." I've applied this same approach to navigating difficult conversations. When I know I will be engaged in a conversation where a topic is controversial or emotionally charged, I hold off on speaking. First, I self-reflect on what I want to say (sometimes writing it down as a first draft). Then, if there's time, I run it by a friend. Finally, I engage with the potential "critic." By that point, I can approach the conversation with greater calm and clarity. When communicating through challenges, it helps to process your emotions first with yourself, then with people you trust.

Leave Your Comfort Zone

Sometimes, you need to leave your environment to expand your perspective. When I travel, I'm often in new and unfamiliar territory, and I know *I* am an outsider. The best approach is to listen, respect, and learn from the people and cultures around me. Mark Twain put it perfectly:

> Travel is fatal to prejudice, bigotry and narrow-mindedness, and many of our people need it sorely on these accounts. Broad, wholesome, charitable views of men and things can not be acquired by vegetating in one little corner of the earth all one's lifetime.[2]

The next time you find yourself in a new environment, try approaching people with a friendly smile and curiosity. They'll probably sense you're not a local and might take you under their wing, inviting more opportunities for Big Talk.

Find Commonalities Across Divides

One of the most common questions people ask about Big Talk is "How do you navigate conversations when people have different political views?" My answer: Don't start with politics, and avoid leading with divisive statements. When someone shares their beliefs, I usually don't state mine outright unless they ask or the conversation naturally leads there.

Instead, focus on understanding where the other person is coming from—their background, life experiences, and what shaped their worldview. Judging someone solely by their political stance before knowing their story is like judging a book by its cover—you might miss out on the depth within. Look for synchronicity—shared values or experiences you can build upon. Start with common ground: a favorite hiking trail, a love for jazz, or cherished wisdom from grandparents.

Tough political conversations, especially when emotions run high, require careful navigation. Think of it like a mediated discussion—having a neutral guide can keep things respectful and productive. Shows like NPR's *Left, Right & Center* demonstrate how political debates can remain thoughtful and civil when managed well. Without this kind of balance, conversations can quickly spiral into chaos, derailing any chance for meaningful dialogue.

The key is patience, empathy, and a genuine intent to understand—not just to win. When approached this way, the most challenging political conversations can lead to greater understanding, even if agreement isn't reached.

Slow Down the Fire

Chris Voss, a former FBI hostage negotiator, reminds us that time is a powerful tool in conflict resolution:

"The passage of time [is] one of the most important tools for a negotiator. When you slow the process down, you also calm it down."[3]

Just as a fire can destroy a forest in minutes, a single heated conversation can undo years of trust. Slowing down allows us to separate emotion from the problem and approach the situation clearly.

That's why people often say things like "You should sleep on it and come back to it in the morning" and "Time heals all wounds." Conflict often feels urgent and heated, but giving space to emotions and reactions can prevent escalation.

Avoid Assuming the Worst

One time, I felt a close friend had grown distant. I texted her a couple of times, and she didn't respond. I assumed the worst: We were drifting apart, or she didn't care about our friendship anymore. A year later, when we reconnected, I learned she had been going through a stressful time. The issue wasn't her; it was me building assumptions instead of taking the time to truly check in on her.

This experience taught me to pause and, in the future, ask myself, "What's really going on here?" when something felt off with a friend or family member. Then, I could take time to check in on them and make Big Talk.

Sometimes, when we think we conflict with others, we imagine the situation as worse than it is. We imagine a worst-case scenario encounter or conversation. However, instead of letting it build up in our heads, if we just talk to the person directly with vulnerability and honesty, we could resolve the perceived conflict in minutes and find inner peace.

Before assigning blame or jumping to conclusions, take a step back. Conflict often arises not from reality but from our stories about reality.

Designate Space for Conflict and Space for Connection

Just as athletes need spaces to release pent-up energy—like boxing rings or football fields—creating outlets for emotional release can make navigating complex conversations more manageable. These outlets could include conflict-resolution sessions, open mics, or even outdoor team-building activities. The key is to designate time and space for these releases. When moments of tension are properly channeled, they bring clarity, reduce the chance of misunderstandings, and help people stay grounded during heated exchanges.

After that particular U.S. election, I watched families, friendships, and communities splinter over political differences. Even my extended family group chat went silent for months after a disagreement. My cousin's solution was simple but effective: He created a new chat with a clear purpose. His first message read, "This group chat is for sharing good news and family events. Political conversations can be handled one-on-one, face-to-face." This clarity helped the group reconnect and refocus on shared values, like celebrating milestones and supporting one another. Heated exchanges cooled off when handled one-on-one.

Practice Curiosity Over Judgment

During that same divisive time, I listened to a heated conversation between two family friends—one a business owner, the other an educator. After the evening was complete, neither mind was changed, and instead, they had been pulled away from the festivities and conversations of the rest of the group, missing the bulk of the evening. The next night, I suggested a round of Big Talk. Instead of focusing on their differences, they answered questions like "What changes do you hope to see in the world in your lifetime?" and "What do you know now that you wish you knew earlier in life?"

The conversations that night were far more profound and came from a place of personal depth of experience and understanding. They shared personal stories, found common ground, and left the conversation with more respect for each other. When we approach conflict with curiosity instead of judgment, we open the door to connection rather than division.

Walk It Out

Sometimes, the most difficult conversations are the vulnerable ones with the people we're closest to. I find it helps to have these talks while walking—moving through our emotions side by side, without the added pressure and intensity of face-to-face communication. If it's not an in-person conversation, sometimes I'll still go on a walk and talk to them on the phone. There's something about the rhythm of walking that makes the hardest conversations feel a little lighter.

Framework for Navigating Conflict

Here are strategies to guide you through challenging conversations where people have opposing aims:

1. Separate your emotions and find common ground.

Take time alone to cool off and process your emotions before starting a conversation and seeking a solution.

- Process your most heated emotions before the conversation (by giving it time, writing a Lincoln Letter, etc.)
- Agree on standards for how you will resolve the issue.
- Listen to the background story to understand why people are interested in their proposed solution.
- Work together to find a compromise.

2. Ask thoughtful and empathetic questions.

Empathy doesn't mean agreeing with someone—it means trying to understand their perspective. Ask them about their experiences and beliefs, and share your own vulnerabilities. Use questions to build empathy and understanding:

- "What's your perspective on this situation?"
- "What personal experiences have shaped your views?"
- "What outcome are you hoping for?"

3. Practice active listening.

True listening means:

- Hearing their words without formulating your response in advance.
- Reflecting back to them what you've understood to ensure clarity.
- Listening to *understand*, not to be argumentative or right.

4. Cool down when needed.

If a conversation gets heated, take a break. Get fresh air, go for a walk, engage in a relaxing activity, or revisit the topic later. Cooling down allows both parties to gain perspective.

5. Find common ground.

Ask each other:

- "What are our shared values?"
- "What do we both want to achieve?"
- "What nonpolitical interests can we focus on together?"

6. Deliver the compliment sandwich.

When delivering difficult feedback, wrap it in positivity:

- Start with a compliment.
- Offer constructive feedback.
- End with encouragement.

For example: "I love the colors you chose for this design. Adding a focal point in the foreground might make it even stronger, but overall, it's bright and beautiful!"

Negative feedback can be crushing. The compliment sandwich aims to sandwich feedback between two positive and genuine comments, ensuring that the recipient feels encouraged and motivated. This strategy is valuable with friends, colleagues, and students.

7. Follow a structure.

When dealing with recurring conflict, especially in groups or families, consider these strategies:

- **Set ground rules:** For example, designate specific spaces or times as politics-free zones.
- **Encourage diverse perspectives:** Attend cultural events or activities together to broaden everyone's understanding.
- **Facilitate structured debates:** Use a neutral moderator to keep discussions respectful and productive.

8. See the bigger picture.

Have you ever watched a documentary about a person who is typically portrayed negatively in the media and then started to feel empathy for them once you knew their backstory—the bigger picture? Knowing someone's story is powerful. It allows us to understand their place in the universe and why they are the way they are.

How we approach conflict—whether with fear, hatred, optimism, or hope—can affect our immediate relationships and our relationship with the world. Conflict can lead to growth, understanding, and profound connection, but only if we have an open and optimistic mindset.

Summary

As you face communication challenges, remember to approach people with curiosity and empathy instead of judgment. To find common ground, prioritize discussing similar interests and shared values. Be open to breaks, self-reflection, and active listening. Conflict isn't just something to overcome; it's an opportunity to connect and grow.

CHALLENGE: EMBRACE CONFLICT

1. Identify someone you have been in conflict with.
2. Choose a neutral meeting space.
3. Come up with a shared goal, such as better understanding each other's perspectives or reaching a win-win solution.
4. Take turns asking Big Talk questions (see below).
5. Brainstorm ideas and solutions and devise an actionable step you can both take.

BIG TALK QUESTIONS FOR NAVIGATING CHALLENGING CONVERSATIONS:

1. How are you feeling right now?
2. What is the most important thing to you in this situation?
3. What is something you would like me to understand about your perspective?
4. How can we work together to move forward from here?
5. What can we both learn from this experience?

14

Be the First to Say Something

The man who asks a question is a fool for a minute; the man who does not ask is a fool for a lifetime.

—CONFUCIUS

When I first started Big Talk, I was hesitant to approach people. I'd often linger in a corner, gathering courage to make the first move. I almost gave up on the project until, one day, I hesitantly walked up to a man in a suit who seemed too busy to be bothered. He told me he had five minutes to chat. But once we started talking, he broke down crying and shared that he wished he had spent more time with his family instead of working. Those five minutes turned into fifteen. Our interaction taught me to always prioritize relationships over work. That one conversation pushed me down the path I still walk to this day. I'm glad I said something first.

We still have the teddy bear.

I once saw a woman named Julie sitting on a bench talking animatedly to a group of tourists. I sensed she was a friendly local with many stories to share. After the tourists had left, I sat down on the bench next to her. We chatted, and she said she had been through quite a lot:

> **Big Talk:** *What have you been through, and how did you get through it?*
>
> **Julie:** *The entirety of my marriage. My husband was an alcoholic. He was abusive. We got up and left one morning. I put the kids on the school bus and said, "We're not going home." If there's anything you want to bring, take it in your backpack. But they were scared, because they didn't want him to see that they might have known. The older two just chose not to take anything with them. And the younger one, I didn't say anything, he was only nine.*
>
> *So I got his teddy bear, and I took it in my purse. And my husband would check my purse every day, but I already knew what to tell him when he checked because the bear had a little rip in its neck. And I told him I was taking it to get it repaired. So that was the only important thing I could think of that we had to*

have, which was the teddy bear, and we still got it. I feel like there's so much we learned as a family.

Big Talk: *What's your next adventure?*

Julie: *I married at eighteen. I never dated before that, and I've never gone out on an actual date.*

Big Talk: *Do you know what qualities you look for in your future partner?*

Julie: *Mostly just to be able to share from the heart. Big Talk, the big things. I don't have time for small talk. I haven't said any of that to anybody. I needed to meet you today!*

After Julie had shared her story with me, she reached out a few months later and told me she had met someone and been on a few dates with him! She felt that opening up to me, sharing her story out loud, and speaking up was the first step.

Her story also touched my life and reminded me of how much depth of experience the people around us have. Courage shines through in the quiet moments we don't always see. You can never know what someone has been through unless they tell you firsthand and share their heart with you.

A year later, Julie told me that she brought out Big Talk questions with her family over Thanksgiving, and it was the first time she had seen her youngest son open up so much.

Being the first to say something can transform a chance encounter into a lasting friendship. Many of us hesitate to make a first move in conversation. We might fear awkwardness, rejection, or judgment. We don't realize how much a small act of reaching out can mean. A study in an article called "Mistakenly Seeking Solitude" by Nicholas Epley and Juliana Schroeder sheds light on this hesitation.[1] In their research, train commuters were assigned one of three conditions: remain silent, talk to people around them, or behave as they usually would.

Most participants assumed others would prefer to be left alone and that they wouldn't enjoy talking with strangers. However, the results showed that those who started conversations felt happier than those who remained silent. While participants estimated that fewer than 50 percent of their fellow commuters would appreciate being approached, almost 100 percent of those who were approached welcomed the interaction. This disconnect between perception and reality reveals a pearl of insight: Although silence may feel safer, speaking up and creating opportunities for connection lead to greater happiness for both parties!

Here are some tips for speaking up.

Say What You're Thinking Out Loud

One afternoon, while waiting in line at a shipping store, I noticed the stifling silence. The workers and other customers seemed bored. One worker had his headphones on. After a few minutes, I said aloud, "This place needs some music, doesn't it!" The worker with the headphones grinned, laughed, and replied, "I don't think you'd want to hear what I'm listening to."

A simple comment led to a lively discussion about music preferences and playlists. It transformed a dull moment into a warm one with connection. By choosing to speak up instead of remaining silent, I created a moment of joy that (hopefully) brightened both of our days.

Appreciate the Humans Behind the Counter

Whenever possible, I try to recognize and appreciate the people who haven't been replaced by machines. If I have the option to check out with a real person instead of a self-checkout, I choose to go up to them and make the most of that small moment of connection. I look them in the eye and ask a curious human question. At my favorite art store, I'll say, "Working on any new projects lately?" Once, a cashier's face lit up as he told me about his dream to turn old bills into a papier-mâché masterpiece. At a morning visit to my local grocery store, I might ask, "Did you have an early start today?" followed by "I hope you get to enjoy the sunshine—anything you're looking forward to after work?" These small exchanges remind us that every person—no matter their job—is a whole human being with stories, passions, and dreams beyond their work.

Follow Up After Meeting Someone

On a sunny vacation in Waikiki, I paddled out to surf a wave and wiped out. When I surfaced, laughing at my fall, a lifeguard paddled over, joined in my laughter, and offered some tips on surfing. We struck up a lighthearted conversation and parted ways.

That evening, I received a message from him:

"I just realized I know you! I watched your TEDx Talk a few months ago and was inspired by your Big Talk movement. It helped me grow closer to my roommate—we started having real conversations instead of surface-level chats. Your talk didn't just inspire Big Talk but Big Actions. Thank you! If you happen to be up north tomorrow, I'll be lifeguarding at Turtle Bay."

That lifeguard's decision to reach out changed both of our lives for the better. We met up the next day and had dinner together, and today, he's someone I visit with every time I travel to Hawaii.

Help Others to Open Up

Sometimes, making the first move can be really life-changing.

Some time ago, I received an email from a man who had been incarcerated for over twenty years, serving a life sentence for a crime he committed when he was thirteen.

As a thirteen-year-old, he gave up his dreams of ever having a family or seeing the ocean. He said that during his darkest times, when he considered ending his life, he discovered Big Talk, and it was the idea that gave him hope. He would ask Big Talk questions to others who were in the psychiatric ward, and they would start to share stories about their past. He said:

> *In prison, we have tablets. About a month ago, I typed "suicide" into my search box because I was struggling. What came up were videos for anger management, yoga, and church sermons, but they didn't help me with my pain. I had to dig deep, and I felt no connection to the speakers. I expressed this to my friend, and he made a profound*

statement. He said, "You know why people with an addiction in recovery have a sponsor who is also in recovery? Because they need people who are recovering to show us that it's possible to recover."

All of this led me to discover Big Talk and understand the need for people to have a simple way to communicate with people who have struggled in similar ways. I tried Big Talk when I was in a suicide prevention/crisis ward. I was in a cell twenty-four hours a day for thirty days. I was in this cell, and the air vents are connected to four cells, and the inmates can talk through the vent and hear each other clearly. I noticed that guys would have days-long conversations and not say anything at all. They just talked about nonsense to pass the time.

So one day, I decided to see if I could get everyone in my vent line to open up. I started by asking, "Have any of you guys gotten any good news this week?" And pretty soon, I was doing full interviews through my vent! These were guys who were actively trying to end their lives, and yet I had them in there talking about how it felt to lose their first pet or how it feels to be angry at someone you can't talk to. I learned so much about those guys, and I couldn't help but wonder how much of one person's feelings translate to someone else's.

I was struck by this man's insight. He was struggling, and he realized that rather than suffer alone, he could say something to those around him who were struggling just as much as he was. His version of speaking up might have saved lives—including his own. Well, flash forward: The North Carolina Court of Appeals released this man from prison, and he has been given a second shot at life to find happiness and to help others through their pain.

These Big Talk stories I've received over the years move me to tears and fill me with renewed purpose. They're a testament to the profound connections that can unfold when you initiate a Big Talk conversation.

Summary

If you're considering starting a conversation or initiating Big Talk, don't hesitate—be the first to speak up. You might brighten someone's day or even change their life.

CHALLENGE: SAY SOMETHING FIRST EVERY DAY

For the next week, challenge yourself to spark a meaningful conversation each day. Whether you're in line at the coffee shop, sitting next to someone on your commute, or working in a public space, take the initiative and be the first to say something. Remember the Big Talk principles of active listening, embracing silence, and asking thoughtful follow-up questions. Break the ice and start by asking for help, giving a genuine compliment, or commenting on your surroundings. Then, dive deeper. At the end of each day, jot down your reflections. What did you learn? What moments surprised you? What new perspectives or insights—no matter how small—did you gain? This challenge will help you embrace every opportunity to make a meaningful connection.

BIG TALK QUESTIONS TO START CONVERSATIONS

1. (Comment on something around you). What do you think?
2. What brought you here today? What do you love about this place?
3. How is your day going so far? What's been the best part?
4. What's something you have learned recently? What's something you have always wanted to try but haven't yet?
5. What are you reading/doing/watching? What's a book, movie, story, or podcast that has impacted you recently?

15

Discover Common Ground

Friendship, I have said, is born at the moment when one man says to another "What! You too? I thought that no one but myself . . ."

—C. S. LEWIS, *THE FOUR LOVES*

Finding common ground is an easy way to build rapport, connection, and friendship with someone. Remember that with eight billion people in the world, not everyone will align with you—and that's okay! There are still plenty of people to connect with. It just takes trial and error, a touch of spontaneity, and a dash of courage to find them.

Connecting and feeling connected is an inside job.

I once saw a woman during my sunset walks two evenings in a row. Elizabeth wore cat's-eye glasses, a pink hoodie, red lipstick, and carried a lollipop—her bold, playful style a stark contrast to my minimalist one. Yet I felt an unexpected kinship with her. We both seemed to find joy in these evening strolls, each adding our playful twist—her with her lollipop, me with my Big Talk conversations with strangers. I couldn't help but wonder if, had we met thirty years ago in school, we might have been good friends. That thought gave me the confidence to approach her.

Big Talk: *What would you say if you could speak with your younger self?*

Elizabeth: *I love you. I love that person. I love who she was. I moved to Paris when I was twenty-two. From Oklahoma to Paris! I didn't even know where I would spend the first night. I saw nuns on the metro, and they were laughing, and I said, "Do you have mass?" And they said yes. It was 16 Rue de l'Assomption. I went to their mass, and they had a place for girls. And so I stayed with them. But I would come in sometimes late, crossing myself like Julie Andrews in* The Sound of Music.

Big Talk: *What prompted the move to Paris?*

Elizabeth: *To study mime. Inspired by Étienne Decroux.*

Big Talk: *What would you say if you could share a message with the world?*

Elizabeth: *Have faith in yourself and know you have all the resources within you. You know, we all want* *to feel connected, and learning to love yourself is the greatest way to connect. Connecting and feeling connected is an inside job.*

I was floored listening to Elizabeth speak! I had also moved to a new country when I was twenty-two without knowing where I would live. Although I went to pursue cross-cultural communications research and Elizabeth to pursue mime, Elizabeth and I discovered we had an adventurous spirit in common and became friends.

How to find your people and discover commonalities:

1. First, get to know yourself. Start by understanding your values. Be honest with yourself. Where do you feel truly happy and at peace? Do you love spending time in nature, engaging in organized sports, aiding people less fortunate, or attending retreats where you learn new skills like cooking, outdoor survival, or scuba diving? Reflect on the people in your life. Do they make you feel at ease and free to be yourself, or do you feel like you have to wear a mask around them? Many people involve themselves in social circles or work in jobs where a constant undercurrent of tension lingers. If that resonates, it might be time to reconsider how—and with whom—you spend your time.

2. If you don't know where to begin, begin everywhere. When I moved to Singapore for the first time, I knew nobody and had to start from scratch. Someone gave me valuable advice: "If you don't know where to start, start by saying yes to everything. You never know where one event, connection, or invitation could lead." So, that's what I did. I said yes. I started finding things in common with people and expanding my sense of self.

This yes attitude had me following a trail of passions and connections that led me to join an art collective, attend an event at the U.S. ambassador's home, work out with marines at the embassy, play tennis in a country club, interview Bangladeshi migrant workers for an NGO, salsa dance in a nightclub with friends from Japan, visit Sri Lanka and Bali with new friends, and speak about Big Talk to a Muslim women's organization. At each event, I would meet new people and broaden my understanding of the country, other cultures, and myself. I left Singapore one year later with lifelong friendships and new hobbies and passions. If you have nothing to lose, say yes.

3. Explore new communities and blossoming passions. Once you know what interests you, you can join organizations, classes, and groups that match those interests. Remember: The key is showing up; the rest will work itself out!

Openly share your passions and goals with people, and notice whom you can talk with freely. Pick up on details that signal you have something in common with someone. For example, a woman once offered me some supplies when I was fostering animals. I noticed an aloha sign in the front yard when I went to her home. I asked her about it, and we immediately launched into a conversation about our shared appreciation for Hawaiian values.

When it comes to showing up, consistency is key. Sign up for communities, classes, or workshops, and keep returning to deepen your bonds with others.

4. Follow up with people and find ways to help and collaborate. Stay in contact with people you clicked with naturally. Follow up with them and invite them to join you in future activities. Contribute and offer help and support to people and communities. Stay active and attend groups and meetings to show your commitment. For example, I don't just go to Taekwondo classes. I also go to happy hour with the teachers and students, have delivered a Big Talk workshop to the leadership, and am working on painting a mural for the studio.

If someone invites you to something after you meet them, show up and support them. Woody Allen is believed to have said, "80 percent of life is showing up."[1] Showing up consistently shows your commitment and builds relationships.

5. Don't give up. Sometimes, we go alone to an event, aren't sure who to approach first, and panic. Remember that you probably feel ten times more awkward than how people perceive you. So, be patient, read the room, and wait your turn to enter a conversation. While it may feel opportune to jump into the first conversation you happen to be near, be mindful not to interrupt a flow of energy. Instead, try to follow and match someone's energy. For example, if their body language is closed off while they are animatedly telling a story to someone else, wait until the story has finished to introduce yourself. However, if a group of people seems to be making idle small talk, this is a perfect time to introduce yourself and guide the conversation into Big Talk! Even better, look for people who seem to have positive energy and share commonalities with you.

Be patient. Remember that making meaningful connections is an art that takes time to cultivate. If you don't meet the right people right away, keep looking. Reevaluate, adjust, and be willing to move on if something doesn't feel right. Communities and connections can sometimes form in unexpected places.

6. You can use social media and the internet to facilitate in-person Big Talk conversations. Some people argue that social media is a pool of superficiality and negativity. However, it can also be a fantastic place to make purposeful connections! Social media led me to write this book. In 2023, I met a hospice nurse on Instagram. We both followed each other and "liked" each other's videos. I noticed that she was also living in Santa Monica. So, I decided to direct message her, saying, "It would be so awesome to meet in person and have a Big Talk conversation!" She responded! We met up, and at the end of our conversation, she offered to introduce me to her book agent. Fast-forward to now, and I owe the advent of this book to her.

In another example, I watched a documentary on an airplane about people who lived in Antarctica.[2] I was enamored by a woman who ran the general store at the American base. Her name was Keri. A few years later, I saw her name in a news article. I decided to message her on Instagram. We were both in San Francisco the same weekend, so we met up, and I interviewed her. We then became friends, and I introduced her to the same book agent the hospice nurse had introduced me to! I thought this was a beautiful full-circle moment.

I make this point to share that social media can be a productive tool for finding your tribe of like-minded people and reaching out to those who inspire you from a place of genuine awe and curiosity.

7. Enjoy participating in activities together "shoulder to shoulder." An episode of NPR's *Hidden Brain* called "The Lonely American Man" struck a chord when it was released in 2018.[3] Men in particular struggle with making friends, especially as they age and lead more insular lives. To make friends, one has to put oneself out there and join new communities, which can feel uncomfortable. Some governments have stepped in to help.

In the 1990s, a movement in Australia emerged called "Men's Sheds."[4] Men's sheds are communities designed for men that provide a space for social interaction and craftwork to improve older men's health and well-being. The movement's slogan is "shoulder to shoulder," based on the notion that "Men don't talk face-to-face; they talk shoulder to shoulder." Studies show that men who participate in Men's Sheds felt they had a place of belonging and acceptance in their community, had the means to give back, and were happier at home.

Aside from sheds, there are other instances where people seem more comfortable bonding shoulder to shoulder.

Think about someone you have in your life or someone you just haven't met yet who might be shy or uncomfortable when it comes to face-to-face interactions, but you have a lot in common. Here are some examples of "shoulder to shoulder" bonding activities:

- **Sports:** Playing on the same team especially fosters camaraderie, mutual reliance, and connection.
- **Visiting a festival, parade, or other public spectacle:** Marveling in something together creates new bonds and shared memories.
- **Traveling together and taking road trips:** Travel is the ultimate way to get to know someone and discover their interests.

- **Safety courses or rock climbing:** Relying on one another builds trust.
- **Disaster relief or volunteering:** Having a mutual cause to care for creates a spiritual bond and connection based on a greater purpose in the world.
- **Hiking:** Spending time in nature is a beautiful way to synchronize with someone.
- **Working together on a garden or farm:** Cultivating a garden creates a shared sense of growth.
- **Being in the water together, kayaking, swimming, surfing, or paddling:** Water is great for mental health and a sense of flow and connection.
- **Gathering and preparing a meal together:** Preparing food and "breaking bread" is the most fundamental human way to connect.
- **Building or working on other home projects:** There's nothing like having a finished product to share.
- **Spectating:** Watching movies, shows, music, or sports is a natural way to explore common interests.
- **Ceremonial activities:** Whether spiritual, religious, or ritualistic, these can be powerful bonding experiences.

These activities allow people to bond naturally over shared interests without the intensity of direct conversation, making them ideal for building initial connections. Once you've established that connection, dive into Big Talk. Remember, the most profound connections often come from deeper, less obvious experiences—like having faced a personal loss or shared a moment of triumph in the face of adversity. These hidden commonalities remind us that genuine connection requires looking beyond what's immediately visible and being open to discovering the deeper stories that shape someone's life.

Summary

Meet new people, and aim first to find something in common with them. Focus on discovering shared interests, values, and experiences to bridge differences, strengthen connections, and create lasting friendships.

CHALLENGE: SAY YES

Practice being a "Yes Person" for two weeks. If you see an intriguing ad for an event, say yes and go. If a friend invites you to a screening of their short film, say yes. If a new coffee shop pops up in the neighborhood and you ask yourself if you should go and try it, say yes, walk inside, and introduce yourself. After you say yes, meet the people involved and seek commonalities by asking the questions below.

BIG TALK QUESTIONS TO FIND THINGS IN COMMON

1. What have you been interested in exploring, learning about, or experiencing lately?

2. What are your favorite places to visit or experiences in nature and the outdoors?
3. What activates you and makes you feel alive and excited?
4. What causes are you passionate about?
5. What little things brighten your day?
6. What's a perfect weekend or vacation for you?
7. What transitions have you gone through in life that brought you here today?
8. What are your dreams in life?

16

Be Willing to Help and Be Helped

The best way to find out if you can trust somebody is to trust them.

—ERNEST HEMINGWAY

A single act of service or a meaningful conversation can profoundly change someone's life. I'm reminded of Edmund Burke's words: "Nobody made a greater mistake than he who did nothing because he could do only a little."[1] I saw firsthand the power of how much "a little" could do in January 2025 when the Los Angeles fires devastated homes, livelihoods, and, tragically, lives.

I wanted to find a way to help. So, I contacted people whose homes burned down, offering to interview them for @MakeBigTalk and share their stories to help amplify their fundraisers. I met people who lost everything in the fires yet still held onto hope:

- Willie, a former star athlete who became paraplegic from a drive-by shooting one year before the fire. Today, he dreams of becoming a corrections officer.

- Grayson, a ten-year-old boy who is blind and a drummer, has raised money to provide canes for children in Ghana.

- Ninety-three-year-old Eric, who lost the home he shared with his late wife, Rose. They met dancing at nineteen. He said they "danced together for the rest of their lives" until she passed away at age ninety.

What happened next shocked me! I shared the stories, and people all over the world reached out to help and raised over $2 million in support. One particularly moving story stands out—I'll share it below.

I lost everything in the fire.

I met Mr. Walt Butler of Altadena the day after he lost his home in the Eaton Fire. Under an orange smoke-filled sky, we sat down for a conversation, and he burst into tears.

> ***Big Talk:*** *What did you love and lose in the fire?*
>
> ***Walt:*** *I lost everything. From a guy with everything to nothing. I spent my whole life helping people. I didn't think it would happen to me, but it did. But I have my health and my life.*
>
> *About ten or twelve years ago, I was going home, going up Lake. I saw this person sitting on the bench, shaking. I knew him because I coached him when he*

was in high school. I said, "Where's your jacket?" He said, "Coach, I don't have one." I said, "Okay, I'll be back." I ended up giving all my jackets away.

A lot of people helped me when I was a kid, so that makes a difference.

I used to have a sporting goods store. Then I started giving away shoes, because when I was going to elementary school, I prayed many a day—because my shoes had holes in them—that it wouldn't rain. So, if they are short of money, I give them the shoes anyway.

A young man today drove at least two or three hundred people to see their houses, and I offered to give him some money for gas. He said, "No, I won't take it, Walt, because you wouldn't take it." Maybe he will be my replacement, which wouldn't be bad. You know I'm one of those dumb guys who thinks you could save the world. I'll think that way until I die.

I've been knocked down before, but not like this. Times are tough, but I'm not giving up.

This ninety-second video of eighty-three-year-old Walt raised over $900,000 for him! Even Magic Johnson saw it and offered to help Walt achieve his dream of building a food truck to feed people experiencing homelessness. If Walt hadn't shared his story and asked for help, he wouldn't have received so much love and support—or been able to pay it forward to help others. A few months later, I had the chance to do the same. Because of the impact of my initial videos, I was invited to western North Carolina to have Big Talk conversations with survivors of Hurricane Helene and help raise funds for their recovery. Since then, I've committed to offering disaster relief through storytelling—whenever and wherever I can.

There are few moments more powerful in our lives than when we get knocked down and someone catches us.

Many Big Talk conversations have started with someone saying, "I haven't told anyone this before, but ____." It's moving when someone chooses to be vulnerable, especially when it's something they rarely share with others. Usually, this is because they feel safe accepting help from you.

I have a friend who can be challenging to make plans with. I often get frustrated because they don't follow through. After a few years of experiencing this frustration, I was on a walk with them, and they also shared the phrase, "I haven't told anyone this, but . . ." They then told me about some medical problems they were going through that affected their cognition and ability to follow through on things. Suddenly, everything made so much sense! With that knowledge, I could empathize and go from a place of exasperation to compassion.

From that point forward, when they didn't follow through, I gently reminded them and helped make the plan for us. Once they were willing to be vulnerable and receive help, it was much easier to move from a place of judgment to a place of compassion for someone I loved.

Offering Help Creates Hope

One day, while setting up a Big Talk art installation in Santa Monica that invited people to share messages of hope, I met a man walking with a big, beautiful golden retriever mix dog. When I asked what gave him hope, he shared a story about his twelve-year-old son. Recently, a person experiencing homelessness asked him for money, but he had little to spare, so he kept walking. A few steps later, his son asked for a dollar. Without hesitation, he handed his son a dollar, only to watch his son run back and give it to the homeless man. The man said the moment left him ashamed but deeply moved—it was a lesson in generosity that he hadn't expected to learn from his child.

Then, I asked about his dog. He explained that his other son, who had been attending college in Santa Barbara, had lost a girl he was dating in a mass shooting. In search of comfort, he and his roommate visited a shelter to pet puppies and ended up adopting Charlie, the dog. Since then, Charlie had become more than a pet—he had been a source of healing in the face of tragedy. "Charlie has rescued a lot of people," the man told me. "He gives me hope. He really does."

His stories were a testament to the unexpected ways hope finds us—through the generosity of a child, the loyalty of a dog, and the willingness to be open to healing and connection.

Find Help Through Community

People often need to feel they can trust someone before asking for help. They fear vulnerability and expressing need. The truth is that everyone could use more help from one another, and we could all use a little help in return.

The key is establishing more symbiotic relationships in your life. Even in a teacher-student relationship, we often hear the teacher say that they learn just as much from the students as the students learn from them.

Finding people to help (and to help you) is easier if you already have a community. According to a study, people are more likely to act prosocially (engaging in behaviors that benefit others and foster positive social interactions) when they feel a sense of belonging.[2] Prosocial actions can help people connect with others.

Although society often prioritizes productivity over community, building strong connections is essential for creating networks of support. It's how we functioned for much of history. Sometimes, I wish we could return to a time when people lived in villages, surrounded by nature, and took care of each other. Until then, building community remains an intentional, active process.

How to Start Building Community

- **Get to know your neighbors.** An easy way to start is by offering food or sharing produce. When I first moved into my building, my neighbors brought over brownies. We became instant friends. Now I always bring them fresh-picked oranges. They let me cut fresh basil from their garden. They've attended my Big Talk events, and I attended their daughter's *Phantom of the Opera* high school musical performance. Having neighbors to support and turn to makes life sweeter!
- **Look up when you are walking and greet people.** It's

easy to look down at your phone or avert your gaze. Try doing the opposite and notice who you might meet.

- **Donate time.** Find a local cause you're passionate about and sign up to volunteer, whether it be tending to a butterfly sanctuary, greeting patients at a hospital, walking dogs at an animal rescue, or another activity that piques your interest.

- **Buy from local shop owners and merchants.** I frequent the same coffee shops and farmers' markets. I once made Big Talk with my local honey salesman who supports a family member with a disability. Our conversation touched me. It feels good to help someone when you know the story behind their work.

- **Host potlucks and group dinners.** This is one of my favorite ways to bring people together! I host a weekly group dinner with my friends to watch a silly reality show together. We keep it simple with tacos, pasta, or noodle nights, barely watch the show, and have a lot of fun catching up.

- **Sit regularly outside on your porch, stoop, grassy area, or a park bench.** By staying in one place and engaging in an activity such as journaling, painting, sports, reading, or playing an instrument, you might make some friends who are also relaxing nearby.

- **Use your local library and community centers.** These places are meant for community building. You will meet other down-to-earth people with similar interests.

- **Engage with outdoor public spaces.** Hang out in parks, town squares, nature reserves, basketball courts, etc., and you'll start to run into the same people who also frequent these spaces.
- **Play sports with other community members.** I sometimes play beach tennis with a group or surf in the same spot and run into community members.
- **Organize or join a block party.** Block parties are places to meet neighbors and have a good time!
- **Join a hobbyist group.** I am part of my local beach association. They host film screenings, beach cleanups, International Women's Day surf paddle outs, holiday parties, and contests.
- **Host consistent events or gatherings.** One year after the pandemic, I hosted monthly Big Talk open mic nights. These events were terrific ways to see the same people consistently and build a growing community! People always left asking, "When is the next Big Talk event?"
- **Create challenges or contests.** My Taekwondo studio hosted a summer fitness challenge, which was a great way to bond with other students and have some competitive fun.
- **Celebrate!** Never turn down an opportunity to celebrate with people, whether it's a friend's wedding, a coworker's birthday, a holiday party, or a family member's graduation. These are the quintessential moments of life that bring communities together.

Once you have established community, you can show up for people, and they for you. I often love sourcing my community for help rather than going to the store. For example, when I adopted a kitten, instead of shopping for supplies, I traded advice and materials with friends and neighbors. People were so helpful!

Help Others While Doing What You Already Love

Brainstorm—Is there a way you can combine helping others with something you love to do? For example:

- **If you love the outdoors:** Take underserved kids hiking or teach them a sport you love. Participate in charity runs. Start a community garden. Support adaptive sports programs.
- **If you love art:** Teach classes or host workshops for kids, the elderly, or community organizations.
- **If you love food:** Cook or bake for others. Host dinners. Teach cooking to others.
- **If you love learning:** Teach subjects you are interested in. You can even host skill-share sessions.
- **If you love animals:** Spend time walking dogs at a shelter or rescue, fostering kittens, or grooming horses at a farm.
- **If you love Big Talk:** Bring people together for meaningful conversations.

- **If you love travel:** Do charity work abroad or go on a kindness road trip!
- **If you love performing:** You could act in community theater, read to children in libraries, or perform music at charity events.

Everyone Needs Help, Even If They Don't Realize It

Try this exercise: Stop and look at the people around you. Ask yourself, "Could I help that person?" If the answer is yes, offer your help. Even if they refuse, it might be much appreciated. I have started practicing saying yes when people ask to help, even if it's as simple as offering to help me lift something heavy out of my vehicle.

Here are simple ways to help someone today:

- Ask a friend what they're struggling with lately and offer your assistance.
- Offer to help a family member or neighbor with chores.
- Write a letter or note of encouragement to someone going through a difficult time.
- Offer your skills.
- Buy a coffee, meal, groceries, or toy for someone you see at a store, café, or restaurant.
- Donate.
- Listen.

- Hire someone in need if you can.

- Devote your time.

Sometimes, when people are struggling, responding to the question, "How can I help you?" can be overwhelming. Sometimes, the best thing you can do is show up and offer something—a conversation, a meal, financial support, a handmade card, or another gesture of support.

When you give help or receive help, you welcome someone into your inner life. It will then be easier to share vulnerabilities and welcome Big Talk conversations. You might find someone saying to you soon after: "I haven't shared this with anyone before but ____."

Now, think about this: When was the last time you asked for help? Find the courage to approach someone and say, "Can you help me?" You will find that people are usually more than willing, and your relationship with them will only deepen. You will also delight in returning the favor one day.

Summary

Being willing to help others and be helped yourself is about connection, community, vulnerability, and understanding that we are all interdependent. So the next time someone offers you help, accept it. And when you see someone who needs help, give it. You may never know how much that simple act could change a life—or even two.

CHALLENGE: HELP SOMEONE

Here's a simple one. Find someone to help today. It's as simple as asking, "Can I help?" or "How can I help?" or offering a gesture of support to someone.

BIG TALK QUESTIONS TO INSPIRE HELPFULNESS

1. How are you helping others? How can you do more to help others?
2. What's a meaningful way someone has helped you?
3. Whose help are you grateful for?
4. What do you need help with right now?
5. What help have you given recently?
6. Who needs your help right now?
7. What's a skill or resource you have that you could use to help many others?
8. What's an act of helpfulness you could do today to make someone's life easier?
9. If you had unlimited time, resources, or money, how would you use them to help others?
10. Is there a way you can combine helping others with something you love to do?
11. How have your difficulties equipped you to serve others?

Let Love Lead

The best thing to hold onto in life is each other.

—AUDREY HEPBURN

Every time I conduct a Big Talk conversation, I make sure to include the same five questions:

1. "What are you proud of in life?"
2. "What has been a challenging time for you, and how did you get through it?"
3. "What do you find beautiful?"
4. "What do you want to do before you die?"
5. "If you could share a message with the world, what would it be?"

Over the years, I've noticed a common theme in responses: Almost always, one answer revolves around *love.*

Whether we're still seeking love, cherishing and protecting it, striving to make it last, or mourning a lost love, love is at the heart of so much of our lives, whether we realize it or not.

If you are having trouble noticing love in your life, don't look at the world with your head; look with your heart.

Some of the stories people have shared with me that are particularly moving are ones about letting go with love in their hearts.

You were so easy to love.

I am friends with a hospice nurse who goes by "Hospice Nurse Julie" on social media. She is known for sharing candid anecdotes about what it's like to work with dying people. Below, I've shared one of our most profound Big Talk conversations:

> ***Big Talk:*** *What are some beautiful ways you have seen people live out their final days?*
>
> ***Hospice Nurse Julie:*** *Almost everyone I've seen take their last breath—it's the most beautiful thing I've ever seen.*
>
> *I showed up at the house of this one family in particular. The patient was not actively dying. The wife was there, the daughters were there, the grandkids were there. They were enjoying the day. And out of nowhere, kind of on a dime, he switched—which could have really scared the family. They could have panicked. They could have missed the moment.*

The family just switched gears. The wife got into bed with her dying husband. The kids surrounded them; they let the grandkids in there. All they did was be with him, and said things like "You were so easy to love." "Thank you for loving us." "Thank you for being here for us."

And he died by the end of my visit.

It was the most beautiful thing I could see, because they didn't have to do that. They could have freaked out. Like, even as a hospice nurse who sees this all the time, I was like "Whoa, what happened here? He was okay, and now he's not." But he was comfortable; they were all prepared. They were ready. And they had this fantastic, beautiful end to his life. They allowed him to die peacefully without having a bunch of panic around him. They got in bed with him literally and just started saying sweet nothings to him until he took his last breath.

I couldn't ask for anything more if that were me. Can we all learn to try at least to practice and prepare to have these beautiful moments that, instead of feeling scary, feel sacred?

Hospice Nurse Julie's story teaches a powerful lesson. The family chose not to panic and instead embraced their final moments with their loved one. By saying goodbye with words like "You were so easy to love," they created a sacred space filled with love and connection. Their readiness to shift and let go as needed allowed them to experience his final moments fully, making death feel like a peaceful surrender rather than a frightening event. Julie's reflection reminds us that with preparation, love, and presence, someone's end of life can be honored as a sacred passage rather than something to fear. We remember that at the beginning and the end, love is what matters most.

We sent him home.

I met a barber who goes by Teddy. He told a moving story about giving his friend and client one last haircut for his funeral.

> ***Big Talk:*** *What's the hardest thing you had to do this year?*
>
> ***Teddy:*** *I'm a barber. The hardest thing I had to do was cut a friend's hair. And send him away. That's the hardest thing for me, accepting death.*
>
> ***Big Talk:*** *He was young?*
>
> ***Teddy:*** *Oh yeah.*
>
> ***Big Talk:*** *Have you ever had to cut someone's hair before who had passed away?*
>
> ***Teddy:*** *No, never. To even turn on the clippers and see someone you're used to talking to and they don't talk back was definitely hard for me.*

Big Talk: *What kind of haircut did you give him?*

Teddy: *Oh, just a regular taper. His mom always said he doesn't let anyone in his hair but you. And I did exactly what he asked for. Yeah, we sent him home right.*

Big Talk: *What are some things you remember about him that you love about him?*

Teddy: *He was a guy who wanted to be taught. He was a guy who always listened. I'm not a perfect person—he's seen that in me. But he saw something in me that had a light at the end of the tunnel.*

Big Talk: *What would you say if you could say something to him now?*

Teddy: *Everybody loves you, so rest in peace.*

Big Talk: *What do you want to do before you die?*

Teddy: *I did it already. I wanted to let people feel the understanding of loving yourself and loving others. And so I could die happy right now.*

Big Talk: *If you, Teddy, could share a message with the world, what would it be?*

Teddy: *Just be kind to others. Show up for people who can't show up for themselves. That's what family is: understanding that we are here for each other. I'm not just your barber, and you're not just my client.*

> Teddy performed a final act of love for his friend. He leaves behind a powerful message to treat all people like family.

Leo Tolstoy said, "All, everything that I understand, I understand only because I love."[1] I feel the same way about Big Talk conversations. Here are some of my favorite love-related responses from Big Talk conversations I've had with strangers, young and old:

"What is love?"

- "Wanting to spend a sunset with a person." —A stranger on the beach
- "Love is consistently doing small things instead of the big grand gestures. Love is being with a person in good times and bad times." —A stranger on the sidewalk
- "Love is this right here. I'm not sure if this is for him or for me." —A man living on the street said as he hugged his dog

"What advice do you have for the world?"

- "Remember that real life is spent in the quiet moments with people you love." —A photographer I met in Santa Barbara.
- "Do what you love to do. Grow up to be what you want to be. You can make your own choices, and take good care of everyone that you love." —An eight-year-old girl
- "When times are hard, just hang on to love." —A couple, aged eighty-six and ninety-one

"How do you handle love and loss?"

- "There's no pill you can take for heartbreak. Hope is such an important word. Gratitude is crucial. Marissa and I were married for forty years, and in her hospice bed at the hospital, she took off her wedding ring and put it on my finger and said we'd always be together. I love you, Marissa. Always have, always will." —Jerry, a man who lives in my building who had recently lost his wife
- "The most challenging time of my life was the loss of my wife, Jaime. We got married in the hospital. The nurses and doctors in the hospital put our wedding together; it was quite beautiful. My dream now is to build Jaime's House, a place for people to better themselves." —Bill, a formerly unhoused man I met in Santa Monica
- "If I knew I was going to die tomorrow, I'd get on an airplane to see my son. It's the most significant relationship I've had." —A mother in Santa Monica

Some philosophers argue that we are born alone and die alone, but that is not true. Love is the anchor of our lives. So many of us were born from love. And the lucky ones will die with the comfort of loved ones by their side (as the man in Hospice Nurse Julie's story did).

So, how do we cultivate love? Love begins with attention and grows with communication, understanding, shared meaning, and emotional intimacy. Big Talk nurtures love by giving it a foundation for growth.

Here are some ways Big Talk conversations can help grow love.

Have Deep Conversations on Hikes, Walks, or Adventures

A shared activity, especially in nature, adds an easygoing, flowing, and magical atmosphere for deep discussions. I love making Big Talk with people at sunset because it is a time of closure and reflection. You could ask someone:

- "Where do you find magic in your life?"
- "What makes you feel most alive and connected to the world?"
- "What other adventures do you hope to go on together?"
- "What have you been thinking about a lot lately?"

Practice Gratitude and Reflection Together

My childhood friend and I have a ritual where we text each other photos of "little joys"—things that seemingly are inconsequential but bring us joy and feelings of love. I also ask whoever I'm with at the end of the day:

- "What moments from today are you grateful for?"
- "What do you look forward to tomorrow?"

Engage in Self-Love

Big Talk is just as much about falling in love with yourself as it is about falling in love with humanity. I highly encourage you to practice journaling and answer questions like:

- "What do you love about yourself?"
- "What are you proud of?"
- "What are your wildest dreams?"
- "What have you overcome?"

Ask Big Talk Questions at Intimate Gatherings

Many people have shared Big Talk questions that helped them cultivate meaningful conversations at gatherings with family members and friends. When asked around the living room or dinner table, Big Talk can enhance conversations with questions such as:

- "What is something you have always wanted to do that you haven't given yourself permission to do?"
- "What are some stories from your family history that you are proud of?"
- "What new traditions can we cultivate together?"
- "What makes you feel loved?"

Reflect During Holidays, Celebrations, and Milestones

Birthdays, New Year's parties, holidays, Valentine's Day—are all moments to pause and reflect with loved ones. You can ask people questions such as:

- "What are your wishes for this year?"
- "What are you excited about for the future?"
- "What can you do today that you couldn't do last year?"

In the end, the most profound experiences in life tie back to love. We find peace by nurturing love within ourselves and purpose when we bring love to the world. We shed tears saying goodbye to those we cherish or when celebrating love between people. Approach life with an open heart, choosing compassion and courage over fear and indifference. Be brave. Ask deep questions and show your true self. When we lead with love, we create a ripple of kindness and authenticity that makes others feel seen and heard. So, love first—and watch the connections unfold.

Summary

Remember that most deep experiences in life tie back to love. Cultivate love by engaging in meaningful conversations and sharing passions and experiences.

CHALLENGE: GO ON REGULAR DATES WITH PEOPLE YOU LOVE

Set aside a regular time to go on a date with someone you love to cultivate your relationship. Choose a theme or question to explore during each date. For example, before I got married,

I would go on "Big Talk Walks" with my fiancé and discuss a different theme for each walk, such as career dreams, travel bucket lists, or childhood memories. I also go on weekly lunch dates with my dad, where we discuss life, work, our shared passion for music, and our family.

BIG TALK QUESTIONS TO CULTIVATE LOVE

1. What does love mean to you?
2. What is a tradition or ritual we could create together?
3. What is a fear you have that you don't often share aloud?
4. What do you love about our connection?
5. What dreams do you hope to achieve in your lifetime?
6. When do you feel close to others?
7. What lessons have you learned from past relationships?
8. Who or what has influenced your views on love and relationships?
9. When have you felt truly cared for?
10. What can we do to continue to grow our connection?

18

Talking to Strangers—A Roundtable Discussion

Through starting Big Talk, I've met others who also believe in the power of a meaningful conversation with a total stranger. While writing this book, I organized a virtual conversation with a few of the individuals I admire for their ability to spark meaningful connections with people they have just met.

We reflected on how talking to strangers is refreshing—a blank slate you don't always get with coworkers, friends, or acquaintances. It pulls us out of our usual bubbles. These brief interactions can surprise us, teach us, and remind us how much we all have in common. I feel like every Big Talk conversation is a gift.

Everyone has their own approach to connecting with strangers—some lead with curiosity, others with boldness or humor. Connection is always possible—and you get to make it your own.

Below is a transcript of our conversation, with some sentences edited for clarity.

PARTICIPANTS

Hunter Prosper—ICU nurse and video storyteller known for capturing the beauty of human connection through candid interviews with strangers

Steph Tonneson—A digital creator who tells stories about mindful living and human connection

Eric Jeng—NYC-based content creator who interviews strangers, capturing their stories to explore the depth and diversity of the human experience

TRANSCRIPT

Kalina

Why do you all do what you do? Why do you spend your lives connecting with strangers and sharing those conversations with the world?

Hunter

For me, I needed therapy—but I didn't know it. I think I ask people the questions I was once scared to answer myself. And then I hear their answers and feel less alone.

Kalina

I agree. Talking to strangers makes me feel alive and human. I need that dose of raw truth and authentic connection. After talking to someone, I feel

high, like I just gleaned some universal truth about humanity. I feel like a rocket scientist! It's a sense of euphoria that's hard to describe.

Eric

For me, it's multifaceted. At the core, it stems from my faith and what I feel I'm supposed to do regarding service to the world. When I think about how I want to help the world or people in general—this is what comes out.

The other motivation is curiosity. What makes people who they are, and what happened to them to get them to where they are?

I love hearing people's thoughts, ideas, and stories and trying to track them. Like, okay, this happened, and then this happened, and now that's why you're like this. And you can find these themes and ideas across people and stories, and you're like, oh, that's how life works. I get it. I just discovered a little nugget of wisdom or truth or beauty.

Steph

For me, it's hearing people mention similar struggles or pains. You can tell a person feels alone. But then I talk to someone else, and they mention something similar. And I just want to tell everybody that they're not alone! I also like the positive and inspiring side of that: Even when people are struggling, they persist. They still find joy.

Kalina

One of my favorite questions I ask people is, "What's been the darkest time in your life, and how did you get through it?" Through all their responses, I now have a little playbook of hope for the world.

Does anyone have a specific conversation with a stranger that moved them or changed their view on something?

Eric

I take something away from every single conversation.

I remember I talked to a guy from Africa who grew up with no food, and now I'm just so much more conscious of not wasting food.

Then, there was a guy who talked about losing his mom recently and his dad about ten years ago. He said he wished he had spoken to his parents more and just gotten to know them. That hit me. So now I'm asking my mom questions like "What were you and Dad like in high school?"

So, it's the little things that may sound obvious when you read about it or watch a show, but hearing it directly from people you're talking with just sticks with you in a way that nothing else does.

Hunter

Yeah, I get something from every conversation too. But the overarching theme I've gotten from all these conversations (and it's more something you just say until you experience it) is that we're all more alike than different.

It's not until you're out in the field meeting so many people from different walks of life that you realize a thread that connects all of us.

And I think that thread is emotion—like, everyone experiences fear, love, anxiety, pain. I may not have gone through exactly what you have, but I know how you feel.

Steph

It was probably meeting a guy named Orly. He goes to the beach every week and sets up a table with signs that say "Here to Listen." He invited me to join him once. He showed me a new approach to listening. He has rules for himself, like "no advice" and "don't ask questions unless it's naturally appropriate." So he tries to pay attention when he feels curiosity come up in him. He asks himself, "Is this curiosity coming from I want to know this, and I'm going to ask a question that's going to take the conversation in a new direction—or am I asking this because it fits with what the other person is saying, and it would make sense for me to ask it?"

It was incredible to watch him exercise such restraint, and the way he did it affected me.

Kalina

I love that. Okay, I'll share one too. I've been talking to many older women lately, like women in their eighties and nineties, who dance, go on hikes, wear lipstick, and are so vibrant. Talking to these women who are so full of life and wisdom gives me hope. I met an eighty-seven-year-old who takes hip-hop dance classes and just got her black belt! That's so inspiring. It makes me feel like I can live fully at any age.

Kalina

Do you all have any practical tips on starting a deeper conversation? Do you have any favorite questions or approaches?

Hunter

I was talking to a stranger, and one thing I learned from him is to let there be silence in a conversation. Give the person space to say more. Because when you rush to fill that silence, you're potentially telling them what they have to say is not worth the time. So, after hearing that about a year ago, I've been more mindful. Before, I was like, "Oh, I don't want to feel awkward. Let's keep the conversation going." But now I sit back and let it get even awkwardly quiet. And then you'll find that they'll say something real. Something they can finally get off their chest.

So that's something I would say. Give space for silence.

Steph

I focus on what people love and what excites them the most. And when I approach a stranger, I'll usually comment on something happening around us, a thought I have that I'll just say out loud. So, at a coffee shop or airport, I'll comment on the music or something going on down the hall and then see how they respond. If they're not into it, I just leave it be.

Kalina

It's like making a little bid for connection.

Eric

Yeah, throwing them a ball to see if they'll throw it back.

It took a lot of practice because talking to strangers didn't come naturally at first. I have a mindset now when I'm walking down the street where I remind myself that we're all connected, part of this big matrix. Some days, I feel disconnected, but then I remember that we're all humans. I can mesh with everything around me. It makes it less scary to approach a stranger and assume rapport with everyone.

Kalina

Yeah. Sometimes, I try to "linger" if I'm out and notice someone who seems interesting. I'll slow down with what I'm doing or hang around a little longer to create a space for conversation. Like this one time, I saw an older woman walking around at sunset. And then the next day, I saw her again. So this time, I sort of stopped nearby to watch the sunset, and when she stopped to watch the sunset, too, I said hello. I've done that a few times when I saw someone interesting, or they were talking to someone else, and I just waited.

Slowing down helps me find and cultivate those conversations and connections.

Hunter

Lingering is a good word for it. You're creating an environment for connection, which is cool. I'm more passive—I wait for a chance encounter to happen—but you're putting yourself out there. A model that I subscribe to relies on chance or destiny. Yours is cool because you're saying, I'm creating the destiny. I'm creating the chance.

Summary

Talking to strangers can make us feel more alive and connected and even serve as personal therapy. The more you engage with others, the more you realize how similar we are, sharing common emotions and experiences.

To create meaningful connections:

- Embrace silence as part of the conversation—it allows for deeper reflection and gives someone a second chance to share.
- Make a bid for connection with a stranger by commenting on something in your shared environment and seeing if they respond enthusiastically.
- Slow down in your daily life to create opportunities for chance encounters.

19

How to Facilitate Meaningful Big Talk Conversations and Events

When I took a leave from college in 2015, I was eager to make new friends in the "real world." So, I decided to cohost a dinner with ten strangers. My cohost and I invited people who didn't know one another in hopes that they would make new connections. I wrote down deep questions on blank note cards for people to use as conversation starters. As the night progressed, people maneuvered around the room, asking one another these questions. They were such a hit that this concept became the first edition of the Big Talk Question Card Game. I have since used Big Talk cards at events worldwide, from Singapore to Australia and Kazakhstan.

Having a spontaneous, engaging conversation with someone on the street differs from facilitating a gathering to create meaningful connections. In this chapter, I'll share tips for facilitating Big Talk conversations at your next gathering or event. These suggestions are based on my personal experiences leading Big Talk conversations at events ranging from a U.S. ambassador's dinner to an evening celebrating entrepreneurial surfers to a UN-themed event for one thousand teenage girls to an artist's launch party at a Los Angeles nightclub to my own wedding welcome party. Learning how to facilitate Big Talk has been an iterative journey, but the core aim has always been the same: bringing people together to quickly form meaningful bonds.

Over the years, guests have left Big Talk events proclaiming:

> "This was the best event/workshop/presentation/party I have ever attended!"
>
> "This is one of the few events I felt comfortable showing up to alone because everyone was so open and thoughtful."
>
> "Something about tonight felt different, like there was magic in the air."

Facilitating Big Talk requires intention, structure, tools, and compassion. Here are the steps necessary to introduce Big Talk at your next gathering:

1. Establish purpose.

Every event needs a purpose. Priya Parker, author of *The Art of Gathering*, specifies that a purpose differs from a category.[1] For example, a birthday party is a category. In contrast, a purpose might be "bringing my friends together from different phases of my life to meet and bond so that we may all share in future life experiences together." Or for the category of company retreat, your purpose may be to "have face-to-face time where my employees can engage in play and get to know one another beyond their professional identities."

To find your purpose for hosting an event, ask yourself these questions:

- What ideas or themes do I want to introduce to the event?
- How do I want people to feel as they leave the event?
- What topics do I want to make sure people can openly talk about?
- Who do I ideally hope will hit it off?
- What emotional experiences do I want guests to feel from the event?
- How does this event fit into a larger narrative? Will there be follow-up events or opportunities for people to connect?
- What are some potential challenges that I can prepare for?

Once you understand the purpose of your event, it will be easier to structure an agenda and activities.

Some events inherently have meaning and purpose and don't necessarily need a serious explanation—or do they?

Once a year, Twinsburg, Ohio, celebrates the Twins Days Festival, where twins from all over the world gather to meet.[2] On the surface, the Twins Days Festival is about creating a fun atmosphere for a unique subset of humanity, but it also has multiple deeper purposes:

1. Meeting other twins who have experienced the loss of a twin and sharing experiences.

2. Learning about medical opportunities to promote well-being and advance research.

3. Giving twins a sense of community, belonging, and identity and learning about resources, including scholarships.

4. Bonus: Facilitating love! Sometimes, twins date other groups of twins based on their shared unique bonds.

Like the Twins Days Festival, your gathering can be a celebration, a party, or have a unique and fun theme while maintaining a deep sense of purpose through the activities you offer and the atmosphere you create.

2. Decide on the number of guests on your guest list.

Who attends your event matters as much as why you're hosting the event. I have led Big Talk events for groups of five to one thousand people. As Parker mentioned, every host has their "magic number" for how many people they'd like to have at events. Here are some of my favorite magic numbers of attendees for successful events where people can bond: 6, 10, 30, 120.

- **6:** With six people around a table, everyone can see and hear everyone else. With less than six people, it doesn't feel like a party, and with more, it might be difficult for everyone to engage in the same conversation.

- **10:** Ten is a good number for hosting because people can often split into two groups of five or fill different sections of the room in smaller groups of two to four.
- **30:** Classrooms, house parties, and workshops/team-building sessions work best with audiences of around thirty. Everyone can meet at least once, and different group dynamics make the atmosphere festive.
- **120:** At Big Talk events, I often divide people into groups of six. With 120 guests, you can divide people into twenty tables. This is a manageable number for hosting a larger event, which is why people often have wedding guest lists of around 120.

No matter how many people you invite to your gathering, your responsibility as a host is to make sure that there are opportunities for everyone to feel like they belong.

3. Who are you inviting?

In 2022, I started cohosting monthly live music events in my friend's backyard. They were intimate, and people loved them! We began each event with Big Talk conversations and then shifted into an open-mic concert. The first event had thirty people—friends and friends of friends who loved music. By the sixth event, someone offered a fancy big house for hosting and the word spread. People told friends and friends of friends, music groups, and artists to attend the event. Those people didn't know what to expect. About two hundred people attended. The event was less magical as a result because some people were there for Big Talk, whereas others stood on the sidelines, confused about why they were there. Instead of a meaningful, curated experience of conversation and music, it became a hectic house party. Through that, I learned that sometimes it's necessary to be more mindful of the guest list. Sometimes, less is more.

Creating a purposeful guest list based on everyone sharing at least one thing in common can lead to the strongest bonding moments at events. Some of my favorite Big Talk events have included facilitating conversations with 1,500 master's and PhD Fulbright students from over eighty-five countries around the world who were all studying a topic of their choice in the United States. These students' purpose was to meet and bond through the shared experience of being alone in a new country for the first time and having a passion for research. As a result, conversations were highly emotional as well as intellectually engaging.

4. Designate space.

The environment might determine whether and how people attend your event. Is it convenient to get to? Is it a welcoming or intimidating atmosphere? Is it somewhere new and exciting?

I've hosted Big Talk events in a living room, a beach park, and a conference center. Each one had a different atmosphere and a different dress code. At the beach, people talked about their life adventures. At the conference center, people talked about what success meant to them and how they had grown professionally over the years.

No matter where you host your Big Talk event, make sure to designate a safe space—a separate area for people to engage in connection. This space could be as simple as a round table for people to gather around or a picnic blanket for people to sit on. It could be a couch, a bench, or a comfortable room with closed doors. What matters is that the energy of conversation and connection is contained in one space.

Having unique activities in different areas also ensures that people will walk around and meet one another based on their interests. Multiple areas for connection can exist within this space. For example, perhaps you're hosting a large gathering in a backyard. Set up tables, chairs, cushions, a firepit, and enclaves for people to connect. Make sure there is also space for standing around.

It's also ideal that gathering spaces aren't spread out too far from one another if you want to facilitate continuous connection. At one event I hosted on a summer solstice, tables were spaced out. I noticed that only the people sitting close to the entrance participated in Big Talk. The people sitting at tables farthest away didn't feel like a part of the event, so they didn't participate.

When I hosted Big Talk at an art walk festival, where each booth was arranged in one line, people just walked past once and never returned. However, at a smaller festival, the booths were set up in an enclosed circle, which allowed people to come up regularly and even meet one another when they came back a second time.

5. Design spaces for meaningful human connection.

Designing spaces that accommodate connection is essential for helping people feel comfortable conversing. Here are some additional tips to keep in mind:

Create an Inviting Aesthetic Atmosphere That Incorporates Nature

- Comfortable seating, warm and soft tones, and natural light can all help a space feel soothing and welcoming.
- Art, fabrics, hanging plants, and decorations can also help put people at ease and provide something to look at.
- A decorative theme can also put people in the right mood.
- Nature also helps people feel calm and grounded, so outdoor spaces, gardens, and windows should be included to help people ground themselves. Biophilic design connects people to nature, enhances mental well-being, and fosters meaningful human interactions. This is why sometimes the best conversations occur in nature, while camping in a forest, kayaking out at sea, or sharing a water break on a long hike.

Organize Dynamic Layouts

- Different seating arrangements and tables can provide space for intimate one-on-one discussions and larger group conversations. Make seating movable. That way, the flexibility encourages people to form spontaneous connections.
- Include spaces for both casual, informal encounters (high-top tables and chairs scattered throughout the area) and others for more structured interactions (such as a larger gathering table). A firepit with seating around it often invites the most warm (no pun intended) Big Talk conversations.

Emphasize Circular and Inclusive Design

- From talking circles in Indigenous practices to campfire circles, sports huddles, and support group circles, circles have been used throughout history to create a sense of community and inclusivity. Similarly, I prefer to arrange seating in circular or semicircular patterns to encourage equal participation and trust.
- Make sure your event is accessible so that people of all physical abilities can comfortably join the conversation.
- Encourage people of different ages, backgrounds, jobs, and life experiences to interact with one another through activities, workshops, and interactive spaces that attract a diverse group.

Nooks for Conversation and Reflection

- Create areas where people feel safe to share personal stories or thoughts without being overheard, like small nooks and quiet areas.
- Include Big Talk question prompts on tables, walls, or throughout the space to encourage conversation and reflection.

Spaces for Food and Drink

- The most primal form of bonding is sharing a meal. Design spaces for people to gather while sharing food and drink.

- Potlucks are often a great way to encourage participation and create a communal atmosphere. You can even have a Big Talk theme, such as "Bring a dish that shares a story about your family," and have everyone share around the dinner table while enjoying a delicious meal.

6. Create structure.

I have hosted Big Talk sessions all over the world (including at my wedding) and usually facilitate each one by adopting the same general structure:

1. Allow ample time (usually around one hour) for guests to arrive, grab food and drinks, and mingle independently. Sometimes, it's helpful to have an activity for people to engage in as they arrive. For example, this could be a guest book on an entry table, appetizers and cocktails, a cooking demonstration, an interactive art installation, vendor and artist booths, photo opportunities, and games.
2. Call the group to attention and introduce yourself. Share a personal story and introduce the concept of Big Talk to the audience (say that it's a movement for skipping small talk to make more meaningful community connections).
3. Once people understand that the purpose of Big Talk is for guests to connect on a deep level, choose a starter open-ended Big Talk icebreaker question to have people ask those around them. For example:

- At a seminar for Fulbright scholars from more than eighty-five countries, I had them ask the question, "If you could create and run a new country, what would it be like?"
- At a Santa Monica city hall meeting during global unrest, I asked restaurant owners, firefighters, council members, sanitation workers, artists, and community organizers to turn to the people sitting around them and answer the question, "What gives you hope?"
- At a party for music industry professionals, I asked musicians, artists, and fans to ask one another: "What is something you want to explore creatively?"
- At my wedding, I asked guests who had not yet met each other, "If you could give a wedding toast right now, what piece of life wisdom would you share?" and "What is a magical place you have visited, and why was it magical?"

4. Then, I ask people to arrange themselves into groups of five to six people they hadn't met before the event (I have found this to be the magic number where people can get to know multiple people without feeling singled out or overwhelmed), and use the Big Talk Question Card Game to open up conversations. Give people a choice of questions, as not every question will resonate with everyone.
   - Encourage people to go around the group discussing their favorite questions and to feel free to ask follow-up questions.

- If there's time, I ask people to write their own questions and share them with the group, open mic style.

Feel free to adapt this format to your use. I have led the same format for Army veterans over a Zoom call, tech executives in San Francisco, elementary school students in Virginia, and exchange students in Uzbekistan!

Here are examples of how you can introduce this general structure and adapt it to different events:

- **Art/paint night:** Use Big Talk questions as creative prompts. Ask guests to discuss their answers to the question with one another and then showcase their responses in an artistic medium (painting, illustration, and collage work well).

- **Dinner party:** Once everyone is seated, open the night with a Big Talk question that each guest around the dinner table can answer.

- **Book club:** Turn book club questions into thoughtful Big Talk questions, such as "How did this segment of the book make you reflect on your own life?"

- **Team-building workshop:** Have employees gather in groups of five or six and ask productive Big Talk questions, such as "What can you do today that you couldn't do one year ago? How do you want to answer this question next year?"

- **Open mic night:** Before people perform, open up the night by asking musicians/artists to meet three new people and ask, "Where do you find creative inspiration lately?"

- **Wedding:** At my wedding welcome party, I gave everyone a deck of Big Talk Question Cards and invited them to meet someone they hadn't come with. It was heartwarming to watch my cousins connect with my friends, and my friends' plus-ones strike up conversations with grandparents and other family members.

7. Use tools.

At each event, I use Big Talk Question Cards to help people open up. You can create your own by writing them on note cards.

Here are some other fun ways to DIY Big Talk questions with tools:

- Write Big Talk questions on different wooden pieces. Stack them like a Jenga tower. The person who pulls the piece must answer the question.
- Put Big Talk questions on cocktail napkins. People can use those as conversation starters.
- This one works great with kids: Write questions on a ball. Play catch, and wherever your hand lands, you have to answer that question.
- Create a Big Talk wall with questions on which people can write their answers.

8. Exercise compassionate leadership.

As a leader, host, or facilitator, you must be a kind and welcoming guide. A host functions as a caretaker, a diplomat, a confidante, and a figurative firefighter. Your role is to be someone people can turn to in times of confusion to minimize any potential anxiety or awkwardness for your guests. Here are tips for being a compassionate host:

- **Be presentable:** Make sure you are clean and wearing comfortable clothes. A professor once advised me to wear blue because it symbolizes trust and openness. I adopted his advice and have a closet full of blue shirts, pants, and sweaters! Whenever I speak at a conference, blue is one of my first choices.

- **Make guests feel valued:** Greet everyone as they arrive with a smile, handshake, or hug (if you know them well)—and make sure you know their names.

- **Encourage inclusivity:** Look for people who might be alone and introduce guests to one another. Try to be thoughtful when matching people who might get along. Also, some people may have different skills or abilities. I have a friend who is part of the deaf community, and hosts sign language Big Talks.

- **Have helpers:** At every Big Talk event, I ask a particular group of friends and confidantes to be my "helpers." I ask them to keep their eyes out for loners so that, if needed, they can engage with them and bring them into the group. I also ask them to help guide conversations toward inclusivity if one person is oversharing or excluding others. Remember to respect boundaries and not force people into conversation.

- **Adapt and accommodate:** Remember that every guest has different needs, preferences, and personalities. Some people need introverted moments away from the crowd. Others might have dietary preferences. If something goes wrong, handle the situation with grace, not panic.
- **Show empathy:** Note people's behavior and body language and check in with guests throughout the event to see if they need anything.

Remember, with all these ideas and examples, to focus on connection instead of perfection. The purpose of the event is to facilitate meaningful connections. Don't stress about details. It will all unfold naturally and as it should!

20

The Big Talk Guide to Travel

Over 1,500 master's and PhD students from over eighty-five countries have participated in Big Talk workshops. I asked each of them to create their own Big Talk questions and share them with the group. The questions they crafted were windows into their diverse life experiences. They also revealed how much we all have in common across geographical and cultural lines.

Big Talk Questions from Around the World

What makes these questions impactful is their sincerity. They are invitations to share something real about the human condition, no matter where someone lives in the world.

"Where do you feel loved?" **—*Argentina***

"When was the last time you laughed so hard you started to cry?" **—*Iraq***

"What has been the most painful thing you had to overcome, and how did you overcome it?" **—*Namibia***

"What is one thing you want to do but don't have the courage to do?" **—*Singapore***

"What emotions do you struggle with?" **—*Serbia***

"Who is the first person you call when you get good or bad news?" **—*Bolivia***

"How would you like to be remembered?" **—*Pakistan***

"How do you hope to make an impact during your life?" **—*New Zealand***

"What gives you hope? What do you hope for?" **—*Ukraine***

"Is the voice in your heart different from the voice in your head? How do you differentiate them and which gives you more peace?" **—*Indonesia***

"If your life story were shared in the form of a book, what would be the book's title?" **—*Uzbekistan***

"What are your regrets?" **—*Madagascar***

"What memory do you come back to the most?" **—*Brazil***

"Define your best day." **—*Pakistan***

"What is a dream you have yet to come true?" **—*France***

"What has been a life-changing experience for you?" **—*Cambodia***

"How do you overcome feelings of loneliness?" **—*Germany***

If you're traveling or living in an unfamiliar place, consider going deeper with these kinds of questions. While it's easy to default to surface-level conversations like "Where are you from?" or "What do you do for work?" Big Talk questions help you deepen your understanding of someone—beyond their title, location, or background.

These questions show that Big Talk transcends borders and cultures. They show how we can skip the small talk and connect with anyone, no matter where we are in the world, by focusing on our shared human experiences.

Instead of making small talk that highlights differences, open up space for shared human truths through Big Talk. You might ask someone, "What is your dream in life?" or "What lessons has your family passed down?" In their answers, you'll discover a piece of their world—

and perhaps even a reflection of your own. In a time when the world can feel both more connected and more divided at the same time, these questions remind us how much we share underneath the surface.

We know only today.

One evening, I received a message from a Tanzanian man visiting America for the first time. He said it would be his honor to make Big Talk. I took a chance and met him on a quiet morning in a park. Kipe arrived dressed in his colorful Maasai warrior attire, holding a beaded stick—a *rungu*, a symbol of his status.

> ***Big Talk:*** *What are you proud of?*
>
> ***Kipe:*** *I'm a Maasai warrior. The son of the chief of my community. I grew up in the place where people call it national parks. It's my home. I live with lions. I come from Tanzania.*
>
> *Unfortunately I cannot tell you my age because I don't know when I was born. My dad never went to school. There were four people in my community who went to primary school. But unfortunately, three friends of mine had to drop out of school because they didn't have seven dollars.*
>
> *So, I found out there are a number of kids who stay at home and don't go to school. So I knew people loved to come to see us and see the animals. The*

job I got in Kilimanjaro, I saved that money, I went to the city. I buy the candy. And when I came to start a school a week later, every morning, they would run to come under the tree because I have candy.

I started teaching them under the tree. The chairs were stones. And I was a teacher. I'm very happy that I can help my community through my passion of guiding, taking people to safari, and Kilimanjaro. But I'm dreaming that in the next thirty years, I can see my community still existing. If we could have girls from the Maasai land become doctors and nurses, they could treat people the same way other people have been treated.

Big Talk: *If you could share a message with the world, what would it be?*

Kipe: *We know only today. We don't know about tomorrow. So what we have, we have to keep for tomorrow. We have to keep for the future.*

Despite our vastly different backgrounds, I felt a deep, spiritual connection with Kipe—one that transcended time and place. Before we parted, he invited me to visit his home in Tanzania. I hope to take him up on that offer one day.

As an impassioned tour guide, Kipe is a unique example of someone comfortable skipping small talk with people from all over the world. However, when traveling, to build the trust necessary for someone to feel comfortable engaging in Big Talk with you, it's essential to understand the nuances that shape how people communicate in different cultures. Before you travel to a new place, take time to ask around and read up on the customs and values of that environment. Once you arrive, practice respect, curiosity, and active listening.

Below are a few examples of cultural concepts that influence communication styles worldwide, offering insight into how to approach people with respect and empathy. Please note that this is not an exhaustive list. These examples are meant to help you understand how to start thinking about navigating different cultural contexts. Awareness of this complexity will help you approach conversations with humility, patience, and a willingness to learn.

Big Talk Across Cultures: Navigating Conversations Around the World

1. Concepts of Time

When I'm on a tropical island, I can lose track of time, spending hours making idle conversation with someone while basking on the sand. I see the world with "island eyes," where every moment, every piece of geography, every interaction is significant and contained in the new world I am inhabiting. Being on an island also creates an island in my mind, separate from my usual reality.

In a bustling city, however, my visits are often for work, and my interactions are squeezed into brief windows—an hour here, a meeting there, sandwiched between busy schedules. Why do my interactions feel so different in these places? It's because our understanding of time isn't universal—it's shaped by the culture and pace of the world around us.[1] Here are some examples of how concepts of time shape interaction:

- **Linear Time:** In many Western cultures, time is often seen as linear, valuing deadlines, efficiency, and schedules. Productivity is the priority—sometimes even over social relationships.
- **Cyclical Time:** In some Eastern cultures, time is sometimes viewed as cyclical, in harmony with the natural world's rhythms. The changing seasons and nature's cycles influence daily life. You may find it easier to go with the pace of nature.
- **Flexible Time:** In Latin cultures, spontaneity and human connection are valued over strict schedules. Time feels more flexible and unhurried, emphasizing the joy of being with others. Here, community is emphasized.
- **Timelessness:** In some African and Indigenous cultures, time is viewed as interconnected. Past, present, and future are seen as fluid and interwoven, encouraging a deep sense of responsibility toward future generations. Thus, you might find more time for storytelling and reflection.

Recognizing these different perspectives on time can help us be sensitive to others' values in daily conversation and adapt our approach to people in a diverse world. For example, it might be easier to get lost in hours-long conversations with someone while walking along the Camino de Santiago in Spain than when visiting a fast-paced metropolis like New York City.

2. Respect and Hierarchy

When I moved to Singapore for my Fulbright research project, "How to Establish Empathy Through Big Talk," my mentors and peers reminded me that I would need to conduct myself differently if I were to make Big Talk in Asia. In many Asian cultures, respect for hierarchy is fundamental. Older people or those with higher social status are treated with deference, often reflected in speech, gestures, and titles.

For example, in Singapore, calling older individuals "Uncle" or "Auntie" shows respect and helps foster trust and openness. This usually earned me a friendly smile and conversation at my local hawker food center or in a ride-share. I also made sure to dress more formally in Singapore (rather than the usual casual jeans and tank tops I wear in California).

I also learned about the "Saving Face Culture." The concept of face (面子 *miànzi* in Chinese) refers to maintaining dignity and avoiding any chance of embarrassment.[2] This might mean someone is less likely to be open about their faults and should not be pressed.

Finally, I learned that certain rituals that might seem ordinary in Western culture can carry more meaning in Asian culture. For example, exchanging business cards is a sign that someone respects you and wants to follow up, while offering you tea or food signifies respect and warmth.

Before or when you first arrive in a new country, I suggest asking a local about the cultural nuances regarding showing respect, as everywhere is different! When in doubt, always ask someone how they wish to be addressed.

3. Spontaneity and Hospitality

When I visited Ecuador, I often found myself salsa dancing and enjoying a meal with people I had just met that day—late into the evening. I loved the openness, spirit, and hospitality I experienced there. Some cultures offer more moments like these than others. In Latin cultures, life is often approached with spontaneity, and relationships are built in the flow of unplanned moments. People frequently engage in open, unhurried conversations as part of social gatherings.

In Mediterranean and Middle Eastern cultures, hospitality is a key relationship-building element. Offering food or drink or inviting someone into one's home signifies a desire for connection and trust. For example, my friend from Spain told me about the tradition of *sobremesa*, where guests may linger at the table after a meal, chat well into the night, and build relationships through relaxed conversation.

4. Spirituality and Nature

In many cultures, spiritual beliefs shape communication and daily life. Understanding the importance of practices like fasting during Ramadan in Saudi Arabia, honoring Shabbat in Israel, or celebrating Diwali in India can help you approach conversations with respect. Respecting people's traditions is key to forging meaningful connections. In fact, when appropriate, engaging in these practices with the people you're visiting can strengthen bonds of connection.

Equally important is respecting Indigenous cultures and their land. Before I led Big Talk events in Australia, the community leader would always begin with an acknowledgment of Indigenous land and culture. I was struck by the diversity of attendees, which reflected Australia's multicultural society. People from various backgrounds often navigate different norms and perspectives in conversation. The outdoors also comes up frequently, as Australians share a deep connection to the natural environment and wildlife. During my two months there, I had the privilege of seeing kangaroos and koalas in the wild! This relationship with the land fosters a strong sense of responsibility, with many Australians adopting roles as land stewards.

5. Shared Experiences

Shared experiences or goals can bring people together in more isolated or unique environments. For example, I mentioned that one of my friends splits her time in Antarctica. She has been stationed at both the U.S. and New Zealand bases and has built a network of community and friendships.

She said that because almost no one living there is native to Antarctica (there is no Indigenous population or culture shaped by history), everyone living on the continent is there as a transient scientist, researcher, or support staff member. People build relationships initially based on their roles and through mutual experiences. For example, many people in Antarctica are there for scientific exploration. Conversations may revolve around sharing goals for knowledge or data gathering. Through cross-pollinating knowledge, people can begin to build meaningful connections.

Since Antarctica is a diverse community of people from different countries worldwide working together, people celebrate each other's identities and work together harmoniously. People also bond over the shared experience of being isolated from the rest of the world and living in such a unique environment (half the year is shrouded in darkness). They learn how to survive together and team up to support one another in such an extreme environment. The upside is the sense of community that emerges, in which people enjoy traditional celebrations such as holidays and birthdays with their tight community.

6. Individualism and Achievement

In the United States, individualism is valued by many. We are encouraged to speak our minds confidently and express our unique beliefs, opinions, and experiences. People are celebrated for their ambition to achieve the "American Dream." Many conversations (and Big Talk questions I have developed) have revolved around goals, personal dreams, and self-growth.

Because of our individualistic culture, people are more likely to live alone and enjoy privacy and choose their lifestyles and interests. The choices are endless! I have friends who appreciate camping, hiking, and natural bodies of water. Yet I have other friends who value material success and luxurious lifestyles revolving around vacations, consumer goods, and coveted experiences. And still there are others who may focus their time on community involvement, whether that means being involved in the government, volunteer efforts, sports (playing or spectating), or local events.

In general, people will build meaningful connections based on their choice of values. Understand your values before setting off to make connections.

Remember that these concepts and examples are meant to inspire you to better understand other cultures before you communicate with them. Show respect to gain trust and open pathways for meaningful relationships across physical borders.

Activity: Your Big Talk Guide to Travel

I love soaking in a new place, people-watching, and auditioning for different lives when I travel. Untethered from my responsibilities at home, I can be a musician sharing songs around a campfire, a confident dancer gliding my way around a salsa bar, or a calm observer sketching scenes in a quiet park with a notebook and pencil. Abroad, I can depart from a more limited definition of myself and explore new places, connections, and ideas.

Traveling is when I feel most free to make Big Talk with people who are very different from me. It's often easier for travelers to connect in a new place because everyone is starting on equal footing. You can make friends on tours, in your lodgings, while adventuring outdoors and experiencing shows together. Even if you speak different languages, music and nature can transcend language. For a deeper experience, consider traveling with a project, cause, or purpose. When I visited Costa Rica in 2024, I volunteered at an animal rescue, and one year later, I fostered five animals and adopted one.

This Big Talk Travel Guide will encourage you and your fellow adventurers to deepen your experiences and create memories through reflection and meaningful conversations. It will add more depth to your trip and strengthen your connections with your companions, yourself, and the new people you meet along the way!

For your next adventure, consider following this set of activities:

1. **Pre-Travel Reflection:** Before leaving, it is helpful to journal and have a "pre-travel" meeting with your companions to set some intentions for the trip. Answer the following questions:

   → *"Where do you want to visit on this trip and why?"*

   → *"Is there anyone you want to meet, a specific experience you dream of having, or a certain place you have been meaning to explore?"*

   → *"What do you hope to discover about yourself, the world, or others on this trip?"*

2. **Big Talk Conversation Starters for the Journey:** During downtime, a meal, or when traveling (if you're on a road trip, airplane, train, or boat), interstitial moments make for quiet times to reflect. Try learning about the people around you by making conversation and asking questions such as:

   → *"What travel experiences have shaped your life, and how?"*

   → *"What have been your favorite moments from past travels?"*

- *"Have you ever met someone new while traveling who impacted you? If so, what is the story?"*
- *"How do you think travel has shaped your view of the world?"*
- *"Where do you dream to visit next and why?"*
- *"What are you most looking forward to on this trip?"*

3. **Engage with Locals:** Make sure to engage with locals on your journey to deepen your relationship with a new culture. Ask questions like:
   - *"What's an event, tradition, celebration, or custom here that you enjoy and find meaningful?"*
   - *"Are there any local legends you grew up with?"*
   - *"What's a common misconception people have about this area?"*
   - *"How do locals (not tourists) like to spend their time?"*
   - *"How can I show respect to the land and people while I am here?"*

4. **Scavenger Hunt:** Develop a list of scavenger hunt activities and prompts that can add color and meaning to your journey. For example:
   - *Visit a restaurant with local color and meet the owner.*
   - *Listen to live music.*
   - *Purchase a meaningful souvenir.*

→ *Photograph scenes that inspire you.*

→ *Take a class.*

→ *Meet a local and swap stories.*

5. **Postcards to Yourself:** Everywhere I go, I buy a postcard that I mail to myself back home at the end of the journey. I write down reflections and favorite moments from the trip. I've collected about fifty, and they make for a highly affordable and meaningful souvenir! If you find a gift shop on your journey, consider buying a postcard and adopting this tradition.

6. **Ending the Trip with Big Talk Reflections:** At the end of your trip, reflect with your travel companions and answer questions such as:

   → *"What moments from this trip do you hope never to forget?"*

   → *"If you returned to this place, where would you visit again?" Or "Where would you visit that you didn't get a chance to see this time?"*

   → *"What did you learn about yourself on this trip? What did you learn about the outside world?"*

7. **Following Up with New Friends:** If you have made friends with locals, consider following up to sustain the relationship. Here are examples of how people might follow up in different cultures:

- → **Business Cards:** *In East Asia, it is common to exchange business cards (mainly in professional settings).*
- → **Postcards:** *In Europe, people may send postcards or thank-you cards to show appreciation.*
- → **Invitations:** *If you made a significant connection or someone displayed hospitality, consider inviting them to visit you in your home country!*
- → **Emails:** *In Western countries especially, email communication is standard.*
- → **Phone Calls:** *In the Middle East, people may prefer phone calls.*
- → **Text Messages:** *In India and parts of Asia, I have often found text messages and WhatsApp to be the best ways to follow up.*
- → **Gift Giving:** *There's nothing sweeter than giving or sending a gift of appreciation.*

If you love to travel but don't have the means, remember there are so many worlds to explore, even right at home. Every new experience, every new person, every new place, and every new event is a world waiting for you to discover it.

CONCLUSION

The Final Question

I was once told: People may come into your life for a reason, a season, or a lifetime. I've found this to be true for Big Talk conversations. Some are brief but impactful, leaving behind a lesson or memory, like processing grief by tending to a garden or dancing at sunset. Others lead to new friendships built on mutual interests—meeting for tea to brainstorm like-minded projects, catching waves together for a summer, or attending a community events series. And occasionally, a Big Talk conversation sparks a meaningful connection that becomes a deep and lasting bond where we continue to shape one another's lives and stories.

If you could have a conversation that might change your life, where would you start? At home or in your workplace? In your neighborhood or on a travel adventure? Big Talk is about more than just asking questions and listening to answers. It's about profoundly enriching lives by choosing to focus on what matters.

Think about a question, topic, or theme that has lingered in your psyche, waiting for the perfect moment or the right amount of courage to bring it up. Maybe you want to ask a mentor for advice about how to get through a devastating layoff, help an elderly or ill family member to check off the last item on their bucket list, or ask the quiet person in your neighborhood what they are thinking about when they sit at that same bench every Sunday watching the day go by.

Why not begin the conversation today? It could open a new door, heal an unclosed wound, or spark an adventure of a lifetime!

Remember, We Are All the Same

When I shared the video of my Big Talk conversation with Bear (referenced in the "Cultivate an Open Mind" chapter), one comment stood out to me:

> I've ridden my motorcycle across much of North and Central America, spoken with people from every strata of society—from government ministers to guys living on park benches—and I've been met with kindness, openness, and a sincere desire to be a decent human being. I've sat with people who vehemently disagreed with each other, and often with me, but I've never been met with hate—sometimes anger, but nothing like the vitriol you see online. Meet people and speak with them. You'll find that we all share similar values, even though we differ in our ideas. If someone wants to be a national leader, they should have to ride across the country they intend to lead. Feel the heat of a summer's day in Arizona. Smell the trees in Vermont after a

> rainstorm. Sit in LA traffic and feel the vulnerability of the poor living on the streets every day. Hear the roar of a tractor pull in Indiana after listening to the Blues in a run-down bar in Chicago. Only then will they begin to understand the people they call their fellow citizens.

This comment felt almost prophetic. Before the global pandemic, I had dreamed of journeying across the country on a Big Talk road trip to find out what connects us. I believed if we wanted to mend the bigger ruptures in society, we needed to begin by repairing each stitch in our social fabric.

After the pandemic, I shifted my focus to rebuilding connections within my community, but that road trip remains a goal. I still hope to experience the richness of meeting strangers across the country, feeling humanity's heartbeat in all its diversity.

If you're reading this book a few years after it was published, I hope I'll have finally taken that trip in some shape or form—and that you, too, have embarked on a journey that brought you inspiration, hope, and new friendships along the way. It all starts with one human interaction. You never know how a single conversation might change someone's life—or your own.

Big Talk's Intended Legacy

In 1977, the *Voyager* spacecraft left Earth carrying a remarkable artifact: the "Golden Record."[1] This twelve-inch disc was humanity's message in a bottle, designed to drift through space and communicate the essence of life on Earth to any extraterrestrial beings who might find it.

The Golden Record aimed to capture our legacy—what it means to be human. It contained sounds and voices from Earth: Beethoven's music, a Peruvian flute song, greetings in fifty-five languages, birdsongs, laughter, and ocean waves.

I hope the conversations sparked by Big Talk serve a similar purpose. While they aren't etched onto a physical disc, they are an oral and visual history of humanity—an archive of our shared hopes and dreams, fears and struggles, wisdom and wonder. These conversations reflect who we are and what matters most to us.

Imagine if Big Talk conversations were sent into space for future civilizations to discover. They would offer a raw, unfiltered window into the highs and lows of the human experience—a testament to the connections that bind us, even across time and space.

Think of the most memorable conversations you've had in your life. Chances are, they were filled with Big Talk rather than small talk—moments when you shared your true self or connected deeply and emotionally with someone else.

Now, think of the conversations you've yet to have, the relationships you long to build, and the communities you dream of joining. These all begin with a willingness to embrace Big Talk.

Big Talk is more than just meaningful conversation; it's a practice for living the most human life possible. By sharing our most emotional and unfiltered stories, we weave evergreen bridges that connect us across boundaries and generations. To those who have shared their stories with me and inspired me, I am forever grateful.

As you move forward, I hope you are reminded that no matter where you come from, you are a child of the universe and part of humanity. Through it all, I wish you the most profound, connected, and meaningful journey you can experience!

BIG TALK QUESTIONS BANK

Below are Big Talk questions you can ask for specific relationships and life scenarios. Feel free to adapt them to your circumstances and come up with appropriate follow-up questions.

Questions for Parties and Gatherings

- "What are some memories you have shared with the host?"
- "How do you love to spend your days?"
- "What talents do you possess that you wouldn't turn into a profession?"
- "If you could throw your dream party with an unlimited budget, what would it look like?"
- (First, compliment them on their outfit.) "What inspires your style choices?"
- (Remark on something interesting you notice about the event.) "What's something interesting you've noticed about this event?"
- "What memorable party or event have you attended, and what made it so memorable?"
- "What do you think would make this party unforgettable?"

Questions for Senior Citizens

- "What's a life lesson you learned through your experiences?"
- "What memories and stories from your childhood and early life do you cherish?"
- "What is a path you considered taking in life but are glad you didn't?"
- "What moments in your life are you most proud of?"
- "What was a dream you had when you were younger that came true?
- "How have your perspectives on life evolved over time?"
- "What advice would you give someone starting out in life today?"
- "What legacy do you want to leave behind?"
- "What is a dream you haven't let go of?"
- "What brings you joy every day?"

Questions for the Seasons

- "What does this time of year inspire you to do?"
- "What is a seasonal tradition you look forward to every year?"
- "What's your favorite thing about this season, and why?"
- "What does spring/fall/winter/summer remind you of?"
- "What's your ideal way to spend a snow or beach day?"
- "What are some of your favorite memories of the holidays?"

Questions About Adventure

- "What are some brave and daring things you've done?"
- "What risks have you been thinking about taking?"
- "What is your personal pilgrimage—your adventure of a lifetime?"
- "What life lesson is this adventure teaching you right now?"
- "What adventures are still on your bucket list?"
- "What's a moment when you stepped out of your comfort zone and loved it?"
- "Who do you want to adventure with, and why?"
- "What are the most beautiful places you have been to and sights you have seen in the world?"

Questions for Kids

- "If you could have any superpowers, what would they be, and what would you do with them?"
- "What do you love to do when you play outside?"
- "What are your favorite things you are learning about?"
- "What makes you smile or laugh a lot?"
- "What's something you're good at that you can teach to other people?"
- "If you could start a new planet, what would it be like?"
- "What message or life lesson would you like to share with or teach adults?"

Questions for Specific Relationships

COUPLES

- "What's a dream we share that we can work toward together?"
- "What nonphysical scars do you have from childhood?"
- "What small things do I do that make you feel loved?"
- "What's a challenge we've faced that made us stronger as a couple?"
- "How can I support you better?"
- "What are your favorite memories we have shared?"
- "What would our dream home/paradise be like?"

FRIENDS

- "What's something you've always wanted to do together that we haven't made time for yet?"
- "What moments in our friendship stand out to you?"
- "How do you think we've grown since we first met?"
- "What's a memory you'd love to re-create together?"
- "What funny or interesting story about us do you love telling other people?"

FAMILY

- "What's a tradition in our family that means something to you?"
- "What's something about our family you're proud of?"
- "What story about one of our relatives inspires you?"
- "What's one way we can create new family memories together?"
- "What family recipe or tradition would you love to pass down?"

Questions About Mental Health

- "What's something you do that makes you feel calm and centered?"
- "How has someone supported you during a hard time?"
- "How do you prioritize your mental health in daily life?"
- "What's a piece of advice you'd give someone going through a tough time?"
- "What's a self-care ritual that helps you recharge?"
- "How did you get through a difficult time in the past? What did you learn?"

Questions About Aging Gracefully

- "What's a piece of wisdom you've gained with age that you wish you could tell your younger self?"
- "What places or communities do you turn to for peace and restoration?"
- "What's a joyful moment you've experienced recently?"
- "How do you define living well as you grow older?"
- "What is your purpose in life? What do you do daily that aligns with your purpose? What doesn't align?"
- "What's something new you've tried later in life that you loved?"
- "What habit or perspective has helped you age with grace?"
- "What activities make you feel younger?"

- "Do you seek to grow friendships with people of all different age groups? What do you find rewarding from your friendships with people younger than you?"
- "What are you excited about? What gives you hope? What are you optimistic about?"

Questions for Difficult Conversations

- "What do you wish I understood about how you're feeling now?"
- "What's something you've been holding back that you want to share?"
- "How can we move forward in a way that feels right to both of us?"
- "What's a way I can make this easier for you?"
- "What's a fear or worry you don't often share aloud?"

Questions for the Workplace

- "What motivates you most in your work?"
- "What's a skill you've mastered that you're proud of?"
- "What's a challenge you've overcome that shaped your career?"
- "How do you like to spend your time outside of work?"
- "What's the most meaningful project you've ever worked on?"
- "What can you do today that you couldn't do a year ago?"
- "What would you be most thrilled to work on in the future?"

Big Talk Guide to Travel

- "What's a surprising thing you've learned while traveling?"
- "What's a place you've visited that changed how you see the world?"
- "What's something new you tried while traveling that you loved?"
- "What's one travel tip or hack you swear by?"
- "What's a trip that didn't go as planned but turned out great anyway?"

Questions for People Who Love Each Other

- "What's a memory we share that means a lot to you?"
- "What's a dream you have for us in the future?"
- "What have you always wanted to tell me but never have?"
- "What's your favorite way to spend time together?"
- "What's one thing you admire about me that I might not know?"

Questions for First Dates or Meeting Someone for the First Time

- "What are you passionate about?"
- "What's a fun or unique fact about you that most people don't know?"
- "What's a place that feels like home to you?"
- "What do you find exciting in life right now?"
- "What are some of your life dreams?"

- "What skill or hobby have you always wanted to learn?"
- "What was a turning point in your life that led you to where you are today?"
- "If you could travel somewhere now, where would you go, and what would you do there?"
- "What books, shows, media, etc., interest you?"

Questions for Personal Growth and Reflection

- "What's a recent realization you've had about yourself?"
- "What's one area of your life where you'd like to grow?"
- "What's a great piece of advice you have received?"
- "How do you stay motivated when things get tough?"
- "What's something you've learned from a past mistake?"
- "What is a fear you would like to conquer?"
- "What is one of your lesser explored talents you would like to develop further?"

Questions for Gratitude and Appreciation

- "What's something you're grateful for today?"
- "Who in your life has made the biggest impact on you?"
- "What's the most beautiful thing you've seen this week?"
- "What simple pleasures bring you joy?"
- "What's something you appreciate about your friends/family?"
- "Who could you write more handwritten letters to? What would you say?"

Questions for Creative Minds

- "What inspires your creativity the most?"
- "What's a creative project you've always wanted to start?"
- "What messages do you hope to convey through your work?"
- "How has your creative style evolved over time, and what influenced you?"
- "How do you overcome creative blocks and 'fill the well'?"
- "What kind of art speaks to you the most?"
- "What's the last piece of creative work you've done that you're proud of?"
- "How do you structure your life?"

Questions for Life Milestones

- "What moment in your life would you consider a turning point?"
- "When have you cried tears of joy or triumph?"
- "What milestones are you proud of?"
- "What's a change you've made that has had the most positive impact?"
- "What's something you've accomplished that you never thought you would?"
- "What's a goal you're currently working toward?"

Questions for Philosophical Conversations

- "What do you think is the meaning of life?"
- "If you could design your ideal life, how would it be different from your current life?"
- "If you could live forever, how would you change how you lead your life?"
- "What do you believe in?"
- "What is perfection for you?"
- "What do you think has shaped your personality?"
- "Do you believe you have a fate or destiny? If so, what is it?"
- "What's your philosophy on happiness?"
- "What's one thing you think the world needs more of?"
- "What does freedom mean to you?"

Questions for Grieving / Times of Disaster

- "What have you learned about yourself and life through this loss?"
- "What is a story about them that makes you smile?"
- "What small things bring you joy and comfort during this time?"
- "What do you wish others understood about the situation?"
- "What have you found to be the most helpful when others offer help?"
- "What gives you hope?"

ACKNOWLEDGMENTS

For over a decade, I have traveled the world, meeting people and listening to their most heartfelt stories. To every stranger and friend who has ever answered a Big Talk question—thank you for taking a chance on our conversation, for sharing your truth, and for offering courage and clarity to others through your openness. You are the reason this movement exists.

Big Talk wouldn't be possible without the love, encouragement, and support of so many people. While I can't name everyone, I want to express my deepest gratitude to:

My husband, James, for keeping me grounded while embracing my passion for Big Talk. Your selflessness, love, and unwavering support inspire me every day. My parents, Wei and Dan, who nurtured my curiosity and passion for humanity. Thank you for believing in me and supporting me every step of the way. My little sister Ariel, my stronger, smarter, better half—I'm endlessly grateful for your wisdom and love. My in-laws, Ivan and Kathy, thank you for your encouragement and support, and my extended family, whose belief in me means the world.

My agent, Trinity McFadden—and Hospice Nurse Julie, who brought us together—thank you. My editor, Lauren Appleton, and the entire team at Tarcher and Penguin Random House, for your enthusiasm, guidance, kindness, and trust in this book.

My mentors, who have guided me with their wisdom and encouragement. To my professors at Northwestern, who believed in me even when I struggled to see the light—thank you. To my Fulbright family and those I met in Singapore and all around the world, for expanding my worldview and reinforcing the power of cross-cultural conversations. To the city of Santa Monica, for your support through programs like the Art of Recovery and Civic Wellbeing. And to every organization, company, and community that has embraced Big Talk—thank you for believing in the power of meaningful conversations.

My friends, some of whom I've known since preschool—thank you for bringing joy, spontaneity, and love into my life. And to those who have supported Big Talk in so many ways—by showing up, offering help, cohosting events, empathizing with a stranger, and sharing in the journey—I am forever grateful.

The Big Talk community—students, teachers, counselors and therapists, musicians and artists, travelers, business leaders, government officials, veterans, prisoners, emergency responders, nonprofit workers, disaster survivors, community organizers, and countless others who have followed along on and offline—your stories, vulnerability, and openness have made this journey possible. Every conversation has been a reminder of our shared humanity.

And finally, to you, the reader—thank you for your curiosity, your willingness to engage in meaningful conversations, and your hope for yourself and the world. This book is for you.

NOTES

Preface: The Big Talk Story

1. Sheena McKenzie, "The Pregnant War Photographer Who Couldn't Walk Away," CNN, February 20, 2015, cnn.com/2015/02/20/world/lynsey-addario-pregnant-war-photographer/index.html.
2. "Adventurer," Dan Eldon Foundation, accessed December 13, 2024, daneldon.org/about/adventurer.
3. Kalina Silverman, "How to Skip the Small Talk and Connect with Anyone," TEDx Talks, Westminster College, published February 15, 2016, 19 min., 41 sec., youtube.com/watch?v=WDbxqM4Oy1Y.

Introduction: Why Skip Small Talk?

1. *Into the Wild*, directed by Sean Penn (Paramount Vantage, 2007).
2. "Social Isolation and Loneliness," World Health Organization, accessed March 17, 2025, who.int/teams/social-determinants-of-health/demographic-change-and-healthy-ageing/social-isolation-and-loneliness.
3. Vivek H. Murthy, *Together: The Healing Power of Human Connection in a Sometimes Lonely World* (Harper Wave, 2020), 13.
4. Julianne Holt-Lunstad et al., "Advancing Social Connection as a Public Health Priority in the United States," *American Psychologist* 72, no. 6 (2017): 517–30, doi.org/10.1037/amp0000103.
5. Tara John, "How the World's First Loneliness Minister Will Tackle 'the Sad Reality of Modern Life,'" *Time*, April 25, 2018, time.com/5248016/tracey-crouch-uk-loneliness-minister.
6. Julian Ryall, "Japan: 'Minister of Loneliness' Tackles Mental Health Crisis," *DW*, April 23, 2021, dw.com/en/japan-minister-of-loneliness-tackles-mental-health-crisis/a-57311880.

7. Office of the U.S. Surgeon General, *Our Epidemic of Loneliness and Isolation: The U.S. Surgeon General's Advisory on the Healing Effects of Social Connection and Community* (May 2023), hhs.gov/sites/default/files/surgeon-general-social-connection-advisory.pdf.
8. "*Mad Men*, Season Two Quotes," Quotes.net, STANDS4 LLC, 2024, Web. 6 Dec. 2024, quotes.net/show-quote/49082.
9. Murthy, *Together*, 284.

Chapter 1: Big Talk 101

1. "On the Method of Theoretical Physics," Herbert Spencer lecture, Oxford, June 10, 1933.

Chapter 2: Be More Approachable

1. Eckhart Tolle, *A New Earth: Awakening to Your Life's Purpose* (Plume, 2016), 191.
2. Dale Carnegie, *How to Win Friends and Influence People* (Gallery Books, 2022), 85.
3. Mary Pipher, *Writing to Change the World* (Riverhead Books, 2006), 180.
4. Yoko Ono (@yokoono), "Speeding up is always the wrong thing to do. Give yourself a chance to go by the rhythm of your own heart," Twitter, January 31, 2022.
5. Hara Estroff Marano, "The New Ménage à Trois," *Psychology Today*, July 5, 2016, psychologytoday.com/us/articles/201607/the-new-menage-trois.
6. Austin Kleon, *Show Your Work!: 10 Ways to Share Your Creativity and Get Discovered* (Workman, 2014), 132.

Chapter 3: Practice Curiosity

1. Ralph B. Smith, quoted in "As Adults We Ask 119 Less Questions Every Day," *Preaching Today*, accessed December 9, 2024, preachingtoday.com/illustrations/2015/november/6111615.html.
2. Epictetus, as cited on Goodreads, accessed December 9, 2024, goodreads.com/quotes/738640-we-have-two-ears-and-one-mouth-so-that-we.
3. Dacher Keltner, *Awe: The New Science of Everyday Wonder and How It Can Transform Your Life* (Penguin Books, 2024), 11–18.
4. Kurt W. Ela, "How to Slow Down Time (No, Really)," *Psychology Today*, July 18, 2023, psychologytoday.com/us/blog/decade-of-childhood/202307/how-to-slow-down-time-no-really.

Chapter 4: Set Intentions

1. Maria Popova, "Thich Nhat Hanh on the Art of Deep Listening and the 3 Buddhist Steps to Repairing a Relationship," *Marginalian*, October 10, 2021, themarginalian.org/2021/10/10/thich-nhat-hanh-listening-love.
2. Bronnie Ware, *The Top Five Regrets of the Dying: A Life Transformed by the Dearly Departed* (Hay House, 2011).
3. Logan Ury, "Want to Improve Your Relationship? Start Paying More Attention to Bids," The Gottman Institute, last updated September 19, 2024, gottman.com/blog/want-to-improve-your-relationship-start-paying-more-attention-to-bids.
4. Gautama Buddha, as cited on Goodreads, accessed May 12, 2025, goodreads.com/quotes/10217544-sometimes-it-s-better-to-be-kind-than-to-be-right.

Chapter 5: Share Vulnerable Stories

1. Regina Brett, "50 Lessons from *God Never Blinks* by Regina Brett," accessed December 9, 2024, reginabrett.com/50-life-lessons.
2. Nikita Gill, Instagram post, posted March 6, 2017, instagram.com/p/DCCMeUwsQX-.

Chapter 6: Listen with Empathy

1. Giovanni Buccino and Mario Amore, "Mirror Neurons and the Understanding of Behavioral Symptoms in Psychiatric Disorders," *Current Opinion in Psychiatry* 21, no. 3 (2008): 281–85, researchgate.net/publication/5470934_Mirror_neurons_and_the_understanding_of_behavioral_symptoms_in_psychiatric_disorders.
2. Stephen R. Covey, *The 7 Habits of Highly Effective People: Powerful Lessons in Personal Change* (Simon and Schuster, 2020).
3. Carl R. Rogers, *A Way of Being* (Houghton Mifflin, 1995), 12.
4. Sylvia A. Morelli et al., "The Neural Bases of Feeling Understood and Not Understood," *Social Cognitive and Affective Neuroscience* 9, no. 12 (2014): 1890–96, doi.org/10.1093/scan/nst191.
5. Samantha Power, as cited on BrainyQuote, accessed May 15, 2025, brainyquote.com/quotes/samantha_power_796826.
6. Mary Pipher, *Writing to Change the World* (Riverhead Books, 2006), 24.

Chapter 7: Speak with Sincerity

1. George Lopez is quoted as saying, *"In life, there's a yin and a yang and a balance.*

And when you don't have balance, you have comedy." This quote has appeared in various public discussions and interviews, although the specific source could not be identified.

2. Alexa Bevan, "Embrace Ichi-go Ichi-e and Live Each Moment to the Fullest," *Rosetta Stone Blog*, February 11, 2025, blog.rosettastone.com/words-beyond-translation-ichi-go-ichi-e.
3. Mary Oliver, *Devotions* (Penguin Press, 2017), 61.

Chapter 8: Self-Reflect Often

1. Gregory N. Bratman et al., "Nature Experience Reduces Rumination and Subgenual Prefrontal Cortex Activation," *PNAS* 112, no. 28 (2015): 8567–72, doi.org/10.1073/pnas.1510459112.
2. Stanford MBA Essay Analysis: "What Matters Most?," MBA Prep School, last modified July 22, 2022, mbaprepschool.com/mba-essay-analysis/stanford-what-matters-most.
3. "Introducing the Eisenhower Matrix," Eisenhower, accessed December 9, 2024, eisenhower.me/eisenhower-matrix.
4. Stephen R. Covey, "Big Rocks," posted August 24, 2017, by FranklinCovey, YouTube, youtube.com/watch?v=zV3gMTOEWt8.

Chapter 9: Cultivate an Open Mind

1. R. Larsen, "The Contributions of Positive and Negative Affect to Emotional Well-Being," *Psihologijske Teme* 18, no. 2 (2009): 247–66, https://psycnet.apa.org/record/2010-23922-005.

Chapter 10: Focus on What Matters Most in Life

1. Liz Mineo, "Good Genes Are Nice, but Joy Is Better," April 11, 2017, news.harvard.edu/gazette/story/2017/04/over-nearly-80-years-harvard-study-has-been-showing-how-to-live-a-healthy-and-happy-life.
2. "Life Expectancy," National Center for Health Statistics, Centers for Disease Control and Prevention, accessed December 9, 2024, cdc.gov/nchs/fastats/life-expectancy.htm.
3. Mark Twain, quoted in *Reader's Digest*, April 1934, "I've had a lot of worries in my life, most of which never happened."

Chapter 11: Practice Kindness

1. Carl Sagan, "Pale Blue Dot," speech, directed by NASA, accessed December 9, 2024, YouTube, youtube.com/watch?v=wupToqz1e2g.
2. Elizabeth W. Dunn et al., "Prosocial Spending and Happiness: Using Money to Benefit Others Pays Off," *Current Directions in Psychological Science* 23, no. 1 (2014): 41–47, doi.org/10.1177/0963721413512503.

Chapter 13: Communicate Through Challenges

1. "Lincoln's Unsent Letter to George Meade," American Battlefield Trust, accessed December 18, 2024, battlefields.org/learn/primary-sources/lincolns-unsent-letter-george-meade.
2. Mark Twain, *The Innocents Abroad* (American, 1869), 648.
3. Chris Voss with Tahl Raz, *Never Split the Difference: Negotiating As If Your Life Depended On It* (HarperCollins, 2016), 30.

Chapter 14: Be the First to Say Something

1. Nicholas Epley and Juliana Schroeder, "Mistakenly Seeking Solitude," *Journal of Experimental Psychology*, July 14, 2014, julianaschroeder.com/publications/mistakenly-seeking-solitude.

Chapter 15: Discover Common Ground

1. "Woody Allen Interview," *Collider*, archived August 15, 2008, web.archive.org/web/20130528130557/http://collider.com/entertainment/interviews/article.asp/aid/8878/tcid/1/pg/2.
2. *Antarctica: A Year on Ice*, directed by Anthony Powell (Antzworks, 2013).
3. Rhaina Cohen et al., "Guys, We Have a Problem: How American Masculinity Creates Lonely Men," *Hidden Brain*, NPR, March 19, 2018, npr.org/2018/03/19/594719471/guys-we-have-a-problem-how-american-masculinity-creates-lonely-men.
4. Danielle Kelly et al., "Men's Sheds: A Conceptual Exploration of the Causal Pathways for Health and Well-Being," *Health and Social Care in the Community* 27, no. 5 (2019): 1147–57, doi.org/10.1111/hsc.12765.

Chapter 16: Be Willing to Help and Be Helped

1. Edmund Burke, quoted in Goodreads, "Nobody made a greater mistake than

he who did nothing because he could do only a little," accessed May 15, 2025, goodreads.com/quotes/90880-nobody-made-a-greater-mistake-than-he-who-did-nothing.

2. Saga Pardede and Velibor Bobo Kovač, "Distinguishing the Need to Belong and Sense of Belongingness: The Relation Between Need to Belong and Personal Appraisals Under Two Different Belongingness-Conditions," *European Journal of Investigation in Health, Psychology and Education* 13, no. 2 (2023): 331–44, doi.org/10.3390/ejihpe13020025.

Chapter 17: Let Love Lead

1. Leo Tolstoy, *War and Peace*, trans. Louise and Aylmer Maude, part 12, chapter 16, The Literature Page, accessed May 15, 2025, literaturepage.com/read/warandpeace-1379.html.

Chapter 19: How to Facilitate Meaningful Big Talk Conversations and Events

1. Priya Parker, *The Art of Gathering: How We Meet and Why It Matters* (Riverhead Books, 2018).
2. "Twins Days Festival," Twins Days Inc., accessed December 9, 2024, twinsdays.org/about.

Chapter 20: The Big Talk Guide to Travel

1. Jelena Mraovic, "Time Orientation and Perception of Time in Different Cultures," *Clockify* (blog), updated May 20, 2025, clockify.me/blog/managing-time/time-perception.
2. "What Does 'Saving Face' Mean in Chinese Culture?," Mandarin Blueprint, last modified March 2023, mandarinblueprint.com/blog/what-does-saving-face-mean-in-chinese-culture.

Conclusion: The Final Question

1. "The Golden Record: Overview," NASA, last updated April 7, 2025, science.nasa.gov/mission/voyager/voyager-golden-record-overview.

ABOUT THE AUTHOR

Kalina Silverman is the creator of Big Talk (@MakeBigTalk). She graduated from the Medill School of Journalism at Northwestern University and received a prestigious Fulbright award to pursue cross-cultural communications research in Singapore. She serves as a U.S. Fulbright Ambassador in addition to her work as an author, video journalist, speaker, and artist. Her storytelling has raised millions of dollars for social impact campaigns, inspiring people all over the world. Big Talk has been featured in *USA Today*, *The Washington Post*, *Good Morning America*, *Time*, *People*, PBS, and more. When she's not making Big Talk, Kalina loves to surf, practice martial arts, paint, write and play music, and adventure outdoors.